Project Management Institute

Managing Conflict in Projects: Applying Mindfulness and Analysis for Optimal Results

George Pitagorsky, PMP

RELATIONAL CONSTRUCTIONIST APPROACH TO RESEARCH

Managing Conflict in Projects: Applying Mindfulness and Analysis for Optimal Results

Library of Congress Cataloging-in-Publication Data

Pitagorsky, George.
Managing conflict in projects : applying mindfulness and analysis for optimal results /
  George Pitagorsky.
     p. cm.
  ISBN 978-1-935589-58-7 (alk. paper)
1. Project management. 2. Business communication. 3. Interpersonal relations. I. Title.
  HD69.P75P558 2012
  658.4'04—dc23

                          2012014271

Published by: Project Management Institute, Inc.
                   14 Campus Boulevard
                   Newtown Square, Pennsylvania 19073-3299 USA
                   Phone: +610-356-4600
                   Fax: +610-356-4647
                   Email: customercare@pmi.org
                   Internet: www.PMI.org

PMI Publications welcomes corrections and comments on its books. Please feel free to send comments on typographical, formatting, or other errors. Simply make a copy of the relevant page of
the book, mark the error, and send it to: Book Editor, PMI Publications, 14 Campus Boulevard,
Newtown Square, PA 19073-3299 USA.

To inquire about discounts for resale or educational purposes, please contact the PMI Book Service Center.

                   PMI Book Service Center
                   P.O. Box 932683, Atlanta, GA 31193-2683 USA
                   Phone: 1-866-276-4764 (within the U.S. or Canada) or +1-770-280-4129 (globally)
                   Fax: +1-770-280-4113
                   Email: info@bookorders.pmi.org

Acknowledgments

This book is dedicated to those who seek to be open minded, to eliminate unnecessary conflict and to make the rest of it productive, leading to optimal outcomes and healthy relationships.

Writing this book has been an opportunity to combine my experience in business, family life and meditative practices, reminding me that there are no clear boundaries between these realms.

Thanks to Linda, my wife, for her support in the writing and editing effort and particularly for the work we have done over our forty-seven years together in mastering the art of conflict. It is through that experience that I have learned that mindfulness, compassion, loving kindness, joy in the good fortune of others and equanimity are the foundation for effectively dealing with conflicts and disputes in the context of maintaining healthy relationships.

Thanks to my teachers and fellow travelers on the path to self-awareness for being an invaluable support system and a vehicle for learning to step back to choose the behavior that makes the most sense for the current situation.

May this book add value by sowing the seeds of wisdom and compassion.

Table of Contents

Chapter 1

Introduction

This book is about how to manage conflict in projects. If you have never been involved in a conflict, you are probably <u>not</u> old enough to read this book. However, if you have experienced conflict and want to get better at handling it, then read on to gain both an understanding of what conflict is and a mindfulness-based way to manage it that combines analytical clarity and precision with interpersonal relationship skills and knowledge of intrapersonal dynamics.

Conflict is a fact of life. People disagree about what they are doing, why they are doing it, and how best to do it. In fact, if you are working in any kind of collaborative effort and there is <u>no</u> conflict, *then something's probably wrong.*

Everyone involved in conflict, whether as a participant, facilitator, mediator, or arbitrator has a role in managing it and can apply particular skills and experience to resolving the situation to mutual benefit.

Conflict Management

Conflict management seeks to achieve effective solutions, encourage healthy relationships, enable personal growth, and support continuous improvement in the way conflict is managed. Because conflict is so common and has such an impact on relationships and results, conflict management is more far-reaching than just resolving or preventing an argument. To be truly effective, individuals and organizations must address not only individual disputes but the environment that gives rise to them and is the stage for addressing them.

Managing conflict well means avoiding unnecessary conflict and resolving the remainder productively. It means being aware that conflict is an opportunity to address long and short term needs simultaneously and to maintain healthy ongoing relationships among the parties. The more you are skilled at using conflict as an opportunity for relationship building and personal learning, the more likely it is that effective solutions will emerge.

There is no cookbook for conflict management. It is not possible to prescribe a formulaic approach to managing conflict. While this might be disturbing to those who are looking for the foolproof, one size fits all approach, it is a reality. There is no one right way to manage conflict. There are many right and effective ways to proceed; there are also many poor ways. Conflict management is more an art than a science; once that is accepted, you can get on with mastering it.

Having said that, at the heart of this book is a singular approach: *Stepping back* so that you can objectively observe what is happening within and around you and the conflict you are addressing. We will use an analytical approach, combined with a healthy dose of intuition, to enable taking a step back so that you can respond rather than react.

Setting the Scene: An Example

There are many different kinds of conflicts in and around projects. They range from small disputes over estimates to major conflicts over project strategy and performance. For example, let's look at a conflict that occurred in a project to implement a productivity improvement tool across four autonomous groups in the same organization.[1]

At the project's start, the project manager described the project, which had as its goal "to exponentially improving productivity and performance." To convince senior management to authorize the project, the project champion project manager expressed this goal in terms of a set of objectives, supported by examples of successes in other settings. Of the four group leaders present, one was enthusiastic, two were taking a "show me" stance, and the fourth was hostile, openly challenging the objectives and saying that there was no way he would ever use a common tool. His area had unique requirements that the tool had to accommodate, and the project team would need to tap his expertise to customize the tool.

As the project progressed, three of the four groups implemented the new tool. That left the resistant group leader and his group.

The project manager met with the hostile group leader. Their first meeting ended abruptly. Like someone who thinks the lunar landing was done on a Hollywood set, the group leader denied the productivity results his peers were experiencing. He told the project manager not to waste his time.

An attempt was made to work around the resistant group manager by going to a few of his group members to get customization requirements. While getting useful information and finding that the group members were not at all resistant to the new tool, passing the group leader only intensified the conflict. He was furious that the project manager went around him to his staff.

---

[1]This story was submitted by Ray W. Frohnhoefer, MBA, PMP, CCP and edited.

The project manager informed the resistant group manager that unless he cooperated, the project manager would be forced to escalate the conflict to senior management. The group manager stormed out of the room.

Senior management was advised of the conflict and, given the successes in the first three teams, put pressure on the holdout to stop dragging his feet and get with the program. The new tool was successfully implemented in the fourth group. However, it took many months to rebuild strained relationships.

Analysis

This is one example of many conflicts regarding imposed change and autonomy.

We said that conflict management seeks to effectively resolve conflicts, maintain healthy relationships, and promote personal and growth and organizational learning. The first goal was achieved; the conflict was resolved so that the project could be successfully completed.

We can't tell whether relationships were improved or whether there was personal or organizational learning. These are the possibilities: (1) The recalcitrant team leader is angry and unhappy, and relationships are worse than they were at the start; and (2) He saw the error of his ways and completely appreciated the new tool and the project manager's patient persistence.

From a learning perspective, these are the possibilities:

1. After the project, the key players (the project manager and the four group managers) meet together, perhaps with a facilitator, to discuss the situation and results to clear the air and learn from their experience.
2. The whole matter is ignored, even during a post-project review, and things go along as if the conflict never happened.

Clearly, this book wouldn't be much help if it did not promote the first possibility. The other possibility is depressing, though all too common.

Process Consciousness and Readiness

Had the parties chosen to address the conflict and its underlying causes at the start of the project, the conflict might never have occurred. It is also possible that the conflict would still have unfolded; the fourth manager might not have taken a meaningful part in a discussion about behavioral process—communications, problem solving, decision making, and conflict management. In fact, any of the other parties or the organization as a whole might not have been ready for that kind of session.

Being ready means having the view that a healthy process can be engineered. People lost in their emotional responses have little or no awareness of the harm they bring to themselves and to others in the group. They will often vehemently oppose looking at the process, holding to their position, in the face of overwhelming objective proof, that it has no substance. Even people who are very good at what they do and are emotionally stable, may not have process awareness. As we progress through the book, we will discuss emotionality, process awareness, objectivity, and positions, how they impact conflict management, and what we can do about them.

As we explore conflict management, we will stress the importance of a conflict management process that balances

- Analysis focused on conflict management as a process, the difference between facts and opinions, the parties' interests, wants, needs and positions, and knowledge of the situation and its characteristics,
- People-centered behavioral skills and awareness including emotional intelligence, mindfulness, and interpersonal communication.

If we balance these, we can avoid unnecessary conflicts and more easily resolve those that occur.

Mindfulness

Mindfulness is the conscious awareness of the thoughts and feelings that are happening in the events (for example, the responses of others, changes in our environment, etc.) that are happening around us and ourselves. We will explore mindfulness later in the book and offer a technique for enhancing it. It is raised as a topic now because it is a fundamental capability that enables the analysis and people-centered behavioral that are so critical to effective conflict management. If you wish to explore mindfulness now go to the section on it in the Chapter 7, The People Side of Conflict Management.

Conflict Management, Transformation, and Conflict Resolution

Now, with a sense of what we mean by conflict management and an example of how it manifests itself in projects, let's explore how conflict management differs from conflict resolution and how, when done well, conflict management can transform the way an organization and its members relate to one another and their conflicts.

Conflict management is as much about avoiding conflict as it is about resolving conflicts. When done well, conflict management leads to fewer conflicts because it explores the source of conflicts and seeks to address the source and preempt unnecessary conflict. It results in more effective resolutions with less effort because it applies the right communication and structured problem solving and decision-making techniques to enable the parties to remain objective and face the conflict with the goal of coming to a resolution that is best for the project and the organization.

Effective conflict management leads to healthy relationships because it keeps people from reactive behavior and encourages them to face the conflict collaboratively rather than facing one another as adversaries. When there are fewer unnecessary conflicts, more effective resolutions, and healthier relationships, there can be a transformation in the way people perceive and behave toward one another.

"Conflict resolution" is about bringing the conflict to a conclusion that resolves the differences between the parties. Resolution is sought because we need to resolve the issues to get on with the work at hand not because conflict is bad. We want resolutions that contribute to project and organizational success.

Note that resolution does not necessarily mean that the parties no longer have differences. In some cases, conflict management may offer a resolution to differences, in other cases, it may enable the parties to reframe their view of their differences. For example, they are able to see beyond them to the bigger picture and, consequently, to put their differences to one side. They may compromise to move on and allow the project to progress, or perhaps one party may defer to the other. Conflict management connotes the *effective* treatment of conflict with a focus on both short-term resolutions and the long-term maintenance of a healthy process. Avoiding unnecessary conflict is accomplished not so much by better conflict management, though it does help, but by better project and general management. Unnecessary and divisive conflicts can be avoided through effective planning and communication.

Transformation occurs when the conflict management process changes the way the parties think and behave. Parties who see one another as enemies and who try to win at all costs can see that it is in their best interest and the best interest of their project or organization to collaborate to seek win-win outcomes. Environments change from being arenas for destructive conflict to becoming collaborative environments seeking optimal performance. Conflicting parties can join forces to address their conflict. Transformation also occurs in environments that see all conflict as bad and therefore try to avoid them. The transformation here is to an acceptance that conflict is a necessary and constructive part of any project or process and that conflict management should be mastered.

Conflict management is often about pragmatism, rather than transformation. In other words, conflicted parties may set aside their differences, but they will often do so through gritted teeth, rather than undergoing an extraordinary revelation in their relationship. However, viewing transformation as unrealistic is a self-fulfilling prophesy. In the end, transformation is highly pragmatic because it fulfills the promise of fewer unnecessary and destructive conflicts, easier resolution of the ones that do occur, and an increasingly effective organization with less stress and greater enjoyment.

Conflict Management in Context

Conflicts are an aspect of interpersonal relationships, and they occur in projects, programs, organizations, the market place, society, culture, and so on. The context or environment influences the conflict. In some cases, the conflict impacts its environment. For example, in a conflict over how best to manage projects (e.g., with greater or less formality), the result can change the environment by changing its governing policies, procedures, and values. Forcing a resolution by authority may forever change the attitudes of the people in the environment regarding their relationship to the organization and their jobs. Consider the impact of the imposition of a rigid and formal approach in an organization that has had a relative loose, ad hoc style where teams adapted their approach to the needs of each project and its participants. Understanding the context gives insight into the forces that drive people's behavior, our own included, and how the conflict may impact its environment.

If the conflict is within a project, how will the organization and its politics, culture, and ways of doing things influence the conflict and how will the conflict influence the organization? Does the conflict's underlying cause stem from some unresolved difference in values or objectives in the organization or the broader environment? How do the parties' history with one another, skill, and emotional intelligence influence the conflict? These are all issues we will address in this book.

Why Conflict Management Is Important: Optimal Performance

Conflicts are neither good nor bad in themselves. Some conflicts cause damage while others lead to the effective resolution of problems. For example, conflicts that pit individuals or organization units against one another can damage the organization by leaving animosities in their wake, while conflicts that pit ideas, designs, choices, or approaches against one another lead to the selection of the best way to proceed and avoid personal animosities. Within project conflicts, when well-managed, provide the opportunity for a group to find better ways to satisfy stakeholder needs and wants and enable organizations and individuals to improve. When managed poorly, they degrade performance and make life miserable:

> . . . a successful team will be comfortable dealing with conflict, be committed to resolving disputes close to the source, resolve disputes based on interests before rights and power, learn from experience with conflicts. These tie in with research on the effects of interpersonal conflict in teams. A team member's commitment to the team and the team mission can increase if conflict is well-managed and resolved, but decreases if conflict goes unresolved. If unhealthy conflict goes unresolved for too long, team members are likely to quit or to search for alternatives (Ford, 2001).

Optimal performance is the ability to make the most of individual and team potential to achieve consistently high-quality results. It is the ability to meet multiple success criteria; criteria that are often changing and often conflicting. This requires an agility to adjust and adapt to match current conditions. It requires balancing thoroughness and efficiency; matching resources with the demands on them. Finally, to be truly optimal, performance must be sustainable (Hollnagel, 2004).

If achieving optimal performance is not one of your goals, then think about that! Are you and your organization satisfied with sub-optimal behavior?

Conflict management is a major contributor to optimal performance. In addition to conflict management, optimal performance requires core capabilities such as process improvement, change management, project management, relationship management (consisting of communication, conflict and expectation management), knowledge management, and problem solving/decision making.

These core competencies work together, like the strands of a rope. Just optimizing one of them will not resolve chronic conflict related issues. Where conflicts are chronic and divisive, it is because there is a systemic problem that involves these core competencies. To achieve optimal performance, analyze your environment and processes, discover the causes of your issues and find ways, within your scope of control, to eliminate unnecessary conflicts and make the rest constructive and easy to handle. This book and the approach it represents will give you a foundation for doing just that.

A Vision of Conflict Management

What is your vision for conflict management?

The vision here is of an environment where issues can be raised openly and without fear, with the intention of helping to achieve mutual goals and objectives and to promote the health and wellbeing of all parties and the optimal performance of projects and organizations. Practicality and realistic expectations are key attributes.

This vision implies that conflict management involves: (1) individuals—those directly involved in the conflict; and (2) the organization or organizations responsible for the climate, culture, and process within which projects are carried out and in which conflicts occur.

The individual's perspective is likely to be more immediate and on a much smaller scale; he or she is concerned with the conflict or conflicts within his or her own projects, rather than the task of improving the climate and success of project management across the organization.

While we are not suggesting that the project manager reading this book needs to save the world and not just their project, we are suggesting that individuals have a responsibility to take a big picture view and contribute to the longer-term health of the environment. For example, having the long-term health of relationships in mind may change the attitude of the individual from "win this one no matter what" to "what is at stake beyond this conflict that needs to be considered in coming to a resolution." Further, awareness of the environmental conditions will give an individual a more realistic sense of what to expect. If the environment is not particularly healthy, then it is more likely that people will be adversarial and less likely to care about the health of relationships.

As we go through the conflict management process, we will point out techniques for addressing the conflict at hand, refer to the bigger picture, and show how changes in it can help to improve the future.

The Rest of the Book

This book is written to give you concepts and techniques that you can apply to make the way you manage conflict increasingly more effective. The book addresses you as someone who is party to or is a stakeholder in conflict situations. You may be or are aspiring to be a project manager, team leader, or participant in any role on projects or in organizations in which projects are performed.

The book is divided into the following major subjects:

Conflicts in projects—to identify the types of conflicts that occur in projects, when they typically arise in project life and which project stakeholder relationships are commonly involved in them, and to discuss what, from a project management perspective, can be done to avoid unnecessary conflict and predict and promote healthy conflict at the right time during the project

Foundation concepts—to identify and describe principles that are woven through the subsequent chapters.

Conflict management as a process—to look at the steps in the process of managing a conflict and to highlight ways to engineer a healthy and resilient approach. Here we define a framework conflict management process that will provide a structure for the remainder of the book. The steps in this process are:

- Stepping back to achieve objectivity
- Focusing on the process to define how you will proceed
- Analyzing, identifying, and defining to better understand your situation
- Seek to understand so that you get to know the parties
- Facilitating to enable clear communication and healthy relationships
- Addressing the issue and its content
- Closing the conflict situation

The nature and anatomy of a conflict—to identify the attributes of a conflict and provide a model for use in analyzing your conflict situation so you can be better informed so you can more effectively accomplish your goals using the right approach and techniques.

The analysis looks at a conflict in terms of these:

- Subject
- Parties
- Decision criteria
- Categories and types
- Attributes

Eight attributes of a conflict are these:

- Complexity: How are the other attributes interacting?
- Intensity: How heated is the conflict?
- Intractability: How resistant to resolution is the conflict?
- Importance: To what degree does the success of the project rely on an optimal resolution?
- Time pressure: How quickly is a resolution needed?
- Certainty/Uncertainty: To what degree can you be sure of the outcome of applying the resolution?
- Reversibility: How easy is it to change the decision?
- Competitiveness: How likely are the parties to be competitive as opposed to collaborative?

Taking the time to go through these lists before jumping into the fray makes a major difference in your ability to address the conflict consciously.

The people side of conflicts—to highlight the central place that interpersonal relations have in conflict management and to provide useful insights and techniques to better manage yourself and manage, work with, and facilitate others. This part of the book emphasizes understanding to manage oneself and others. It is broken into three chapters that collectively address the following:

- Conflict management styles and approaches;
- Cognitive analysis and what drives people's positions;
- Being centered and mindful and what that means in the context of conflict; and
- Managing conflict situations/facilitating rapport.

Approaches and techniques—to identify and describe principle techniques such as negotiation, debate, dialogue, decision making, and problem solving and how they are applied in managing conflicts.

Closure—to bring your conflict to a conclusion, even if it cannot be resolved and to use your conflict experience as a basis for future improvement.

Chapter Summary

This introduction has defined conflict management in the context of projects and project management and provided an overview of the book.

The next chapter addresses conflict in the context of projects and identifies and discusses the types of conflicts we find in projects and how they relate to stakeholders and to project life cycle.

Chapter 2

Conflict in Projects

Chapter Overview

Conflicts in projects have their own unique characteristics but, in general they are like all conflicts. They may be single events or complexes of disputes; they may be part of a larger conflict in the organization, business environment, or culture, or limited to the project itself. In this chapter, we will identify the common types of conflict that occur across a project's life. We will explore why apparently similar sources of conflict can generate different results, depending on who is involved and at which stage in the project they occur.

Exploring Conflict Causes and Types

There are many types of conflicts in projects. Often they appear together as complex conflicts. The more you separate a complex conflict into its component parts of and address each independently, the easier it is to resolve.

According to Thamhain and Wilemon (1975), there are seven types of conflicts that occur in projects:

- Schedule conflicts
- Priorities conflicts
- Resource conflicts
- Technical conflicts
- Administrative procedures conflicts
- Personality conflicts
- Cost conflicts

In addition, we have added the following two conflicts:

- Performance conflicts
- Supplier selection conflicts.

The types are discussed in the following, and as you read through the descriptions, reflect on which are predominant and most impactful in your experience and what you might do to better avoid and address them.

Schedule Conflicts

Schedule conflicts are most common. The most difficult to handle appear during the latter stages of the project when promised deliverables become late. To minimize these conflicts, make sure scheduling is done using a well-developed work breakdown structure (WBS) and that schedules and the estimates underlying them are accompanied with assumptions and risk assessments and include a contingency. Address scheduling procedures early in the project's life. Recognize that many scheduling conflicts are caused by unrealistic expectations that are not challenged at the time deadlines and milestones are set. If that is the case in your organization, make sure that as a project manager you are pushing back to promote rational expectations. Make sure you are asking questions regarding the assumptions that performers, vendors, and functional groups are making when they agree to deadlines. These assumptions regard the availability of resources, deliverables that are needed to meet the schedule and priorities. It is healthier to have a conflict over these assumptions when the schedule is being developed rather than a conflict over why the schedule was not met.

Schedule conflicts frequently occur between project managers and functional managers. We also see schedule conflicts occur between project managers and project staff, between clients and project managers, and between clients. In other words, schedule conflicts occur between anyone who has a desire for something to be done at a particular point in time and the one has to do it, often along with several other things at the same time. Again, it is healthier to have schedule conflicts early on rather than after the fact when the conflict is more about blame than anything practical and useful.

Priorities Conflicts

Conflicts over priorities are most frequent during the initiation of a project where they occur between organization units seeking limited resources and funding for their projects. These conflicts also occur later in project life as new projects arise and as priorities among requirements and activities arise. They may be between project managers and clients seeking resources from functional managers or service providers, or they may be between clients over which requirements are the most important.

Other priorities conflicts may be over the relative priority of the project's progress vs. the welfare of the performers when overwork and burnout are issues. Establishing clear expectations early on (perhaps forcing the conflict during kick-off or setting cross project policies) will help to minimize these conflicts.

Because stakeholders may have conflicting views, techniques that offer a more objective way of reviewing the situation are needed. Cognitive analysis and the emphasis on common interests, discussed later in the book, are means for identifying and clarifying priorities. The use of problem-solving techniques like the weights and scores approach (described in the Approaches and Techniques chapter) helps to resolve these conflicts based on objective analysis rather than subjective opinion.

Resource Conflicts

Resource conflicts are inevitable in any organization in which resources are shared across multiple projects or between projects and operational activities, and there are insufficient resources to satisfy all needs. The number of these conflicts and their intensity can be reduced by resolving priorities conflict through portfolio management and multi-project planning supported by systematic resource management. This may be beyond the current capability of many organizations. If your organization is not there yet, there is not much you can do much about implementing portfolio management and multi-project resource planning. What you can do is ask questions of functional managers and individual performers regarding how many current commitments they have made for their resources or themselves before they over commit.

Resource conflicts may also occur because of differences regarding the qualifications or performance of specific human resources. Project managers all want the same best players and compete for them. Functional managers must "play Solomon," the wise king who applied wisdom to resolve the most difficult conflicts, to satisfy needs, maintain healthy relationships, and utilize all the available resources.

Technical Conflicts

Technical conflicts involve differences over product designs, technical methodologies, choice of technology, and the inclusion or exclusion of requirements; subjects that are directly related to the definition and delivery of products or services. These conflicts usually involve clashes over features, quality and cost, the perceived efficiency and effectiveness of methods, the "goodness" of one design over another. They involve technical subject matter experts, clients, product managers, and sponsors with cost/quality concerns. Technical conflicts are supported by analytical techniques such as decision-making methods that use weighted scoring of alternatives.

Encourage technical conflict when requirements are being discovered, defined, and prioritized, when technical approaches and methodologies are being planned and adopted, and when designs are being created and agreed upon. If these conflicts occur at the right time and are managed to optimal resolutions, they will eliminate technical conflicts later in the project when they are more difficult and more expensive to resolve.

Administrative Procedures Conflicts

Conflict over administration is focused on the procedures and processes used to execute and control the project (time keeping, progress reporting, performance evaluation, quality assurance and control, and procurement, etc.), to communicate, allocate, and assign resources, manage changes and issues, make decisions, and manage conflict. Administrative conflicts can be intense and disruptive if they occur once the project is underway because they get in the way of project managers being able to effectively plan and control the project. Conflicts over administration can be minimized if organizations have well established cross-project procedures and methodologies that are subject to adaptation tailored to individual project needs. With or without these, it is a best practice to raise administrative issues early in project life and to get agreement from all parties on how things will be done. Administrative conflicts tend to occur among functional and project managers and between managers and their staff.

Personality Conflicts

Personality conflicts occur when parties' behaviors and styles of communication clash. They can be among the most difficult to address and they often flavor or cause other types of conflicts. People who may have different styles or character traits that create friction may take a simple conflict over schedule and turn it into a battle royal with the focus on their relationship rather than the content.

Personality conflicts can be avoided by making sure that stakeholders are aware of the basics of relationship management and that they are cultivating their own emotional intelligence. Team building using personality trait and style models like the Myers Briggs Type Indicator will help to turn potential personality conflicts into effective relationships. With less formality, a simple discussion regarding the differences between content and relationship issues can bring a heightened awareness to the team and enable members to more easily recognize when they are clashing over personality differences and thereby pull back to address them in a healthy way.

In some cases, personality conflicts may be resolved by separating the parties or eliminating one who may be the primary cause and who is not ready to address his or her own personality issues.

Personality conflicts often occur during the later stages of projects, for example, during closure or at other times when performance evaluations take place. To avoid these types of conflicts, it is best to make sure that the review process is well planned and facilitated (an administrative issue) and that there is clarity regarding roles, responsibilities, authority and, especially, accountability. Focusing on facts and separating people from their performance and results helps to cut down on personality clashes. The later chapters in this book regarding the people side of conflict management and facilitation techniques address how to manage personality conflicts.

Cost Conflicts

Cost conflicts are often intertwined with technical, schedule, and resource conflicts. It is healthy when they arise early in a project's life, in the context of setting budget constraints, deciding on requirements, design, and supplier selection decisions. If conflicts over costs arise during the later stages of project execution or at the end of the project when the bill is presented to the client, it is a sign that estimating and scheduling were not done well and that project control reporting was deficient in identifying cost issues before they caused conflict. For example, recognizing scope changes that increased costs before they are authorized and implemented will avoid cost conflicts later.

Cost conflicts often arise in the interplay between project managers and their suppliers; suppliers may be internal functional disciplines or external product or service providers. Cost conflicts are healthy when they occur before the work has been committed to and performed. The search for cost reductions leads to greater scrutiny of features and functions, quality levels, estimate accuracy and approach, risks and assumptions, and the choice of technology and technical approach or method.

Performance Conflicts

Performance conflicts are about who has or has not performed well in terms of compliance with budget, schedule, and scope expectations. These may be included in the resource and technical conflicts, but they are worth mentioning on their own. While they may be intensified by personality conflicts, they also exist without them. Administrative procedures, clarity about roles, responsibilities, accountability, performance expectations, and measurement criteria will help to keep performance conflicts to a minimum and resolve them with greater ease if they do occur.

Performance issues should ideally arise close to the time when the performance was experienced. They may be between subordinates and superiors, project managers and functional managers or project performers, or between project managers and sponsors and or clients. Performance conflicts also occur between peers where one party feels the other is not pulling his or her weight.

Performance conflicts include conflicts over these issues:

- Whether a work result is acceptable or not;
- Whether something is a scope change or not;
- "We can do it cheaper (or better) by doing it this way";
- Personality, personal behavior and style;
- Role and responsibility and authority issues, particularly when there was a lack of clarity during initiation;
- "Why was it late and who is responsible?"
- The degree of candor required at performance reviews.

Supplier Selection Conflicts

Supplier selection conflicts are common when there are differences of opinion regarding which vendor to use or whether or not to use a vendor at all. These conflicts may be related to design conflicts, cost conflicts, and schedule conflicts. They are healthy when they occur at the time that vendor selection is being made, as opposed to afterwards when the words "I told you so" can lead to intense conflict that has no real benefit and is hard to resolve. Selecting the right vendor may be critical to project success and therefore healthy conflict that forces the parties to clearly identify selection criteria and make choices that all parties can at least live with will add value. Make sure administrative procurement procedures are set and followed.

Note that conflicts between suppliers and clients fall into the other types. The relationship changes their nature. For example, a cost conflict between project manager and client who work for the same organization has a different flavor than one between a vendor and client. In the vendor-client relationship, the vendor is motivated by profit along with the desire to satisfy the client and cultivate a long-term healthy relationship, and the client by cost reduction along with the desire to get a result that satisfies his needs and expectations. Internally, there may be cost conflicts but they are not made more complex by the profit/cost issue.

Cost and schedule conflicts as well as the other types often arise between sales and delivery teams within selling organizations. Administrative conflicts often come up when a supplier has a different approach than the client.

Project Life Implications

Conflicts occur across project life. From a conflict management perspective, it is best to make sure that conflicts regarding issues like design alternatives and the priority of requirements are addressed at a time in the project's life that minimizes future conflict and maximizes project effectiveness.

Project life cycle refers to the stages in project life as shown in Figure 2-1. More specific life cycle models identify phases such as initiation, requirements definition, design, construction, implementation, and closure.

A characteristic of the generic project life cycle is that "the ability to influence the final characteristics of the project's product without significantly impacting cost, is highest at the start of the project and decreases as the project progresses" (Project Management Institute, 2004, p. 17). At the same time, it is generally accepted in decision-making circles that it is beneficial to postpone binding decisions until the latest possible moment to minimize uncertainty and to maximize reversibility; theoretically, the more you know when you make the decision, the better the decision.

It is necessary to strike a balance that insures that the right decisions are made at the most effective times in project life. To avoid unnecessary conflicts and to

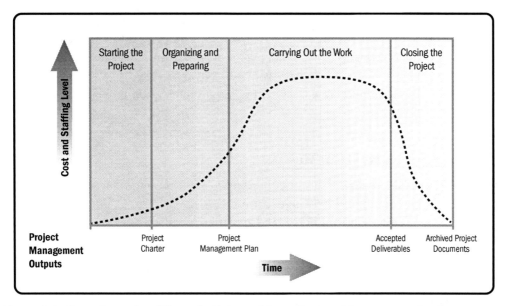

Figure 2.1: Generic project life cycle (Adapted from Project Management Institute, 2008)

ensure that decisions are made at the right time, conflicts should be resolved when the issues are part of the activities being performed. For example, resolve requirements related conflicts before people start buying and building things.

When the sources of conflict are not in-synch with the project phase, it is likely that conflicts will be more intense and more disruptive; there will be a greater tendency for them to become emotionally charged. For example, if a conflict over design alternatives is not resolved effectively during the design phase, it may arise later, during implementation, with a statement like "I knew that design you pushed on us would end up causing us grief. We need to change it now." A conflict like this one could result in bringing a project to a halt while the design of the product is rethought, which results in increased costs and a demotivated staff. If this occurs, the project may be in deep trouble.

Having a clear sense of the causes or sources of conflict makes it possible to "force" conflicts at appropriate times so that they are brought to the surface and addressed before they arise as ad hoc conflicts at inopportune times.

One way of doing this is to make it a part of risk management. During each stage of the project's life, ask "What is the risk of having unresolved conflict later regarding issues that we should be addressing now? What are the issues we should be addressing now?"

Use checklists to make sure you are addressing conflicts at the right time. To "force" healthy conflicts, agree that decisions will only be made after looking at least two alternatives.

In other words, make sure that when you are setting the approach, requirements, and/or designs for your event, computer system, product or ad campaign, you have the conflicts that influence these raised, addressed, and resolved before moving on. If these conflicts are avoided or bypassed because they "just didn't come up," then there is the likelihood that they will come up later when they are inconvenient, costly, and likely to be intense.

Stakeholders and Their Roles

Another aspect of projects that effect conflict is the relationships among the stakeholders. People playing different roles in projects have different interests and levels of authority, different personalities, and different perspectives. In this section, we will explore the roles, hierarchies, and authority of stakeholders. We will defer discussion of interests and perspectives until later chapters where we discuss cognitive analysis.

The typical roles in project settings are

- project manager,
- functional or discipline manager,
- sponsor,
- client,
- performers (with multiple roles including team leads, technologists, subject matter experts, analysts, designers and more), and
- vendors (with multiple roles from sales to technical performance).

A simple mapping between types of conflict and stakeholders is not useful. Conflicts of the same type occur between several different roles, as we saw in the discussion of the conflict types. For example, schedule conflicts may be between project managers and functional managers, subordinates, clients, or sponsors, or between clients and sponsors within the same organization, vying over whose project will be first. Hierarchy, organizational alignment, and authority issues influence conflict complexity and intensity.

In many cases, the parties who are most affected by the resolution are not directly involved in the conflict itself. For example, in a conflict over the choice of a design, the principal impact is felt by the project's sponsor, the people who will be implementing the design, and the sellers and users of the product being designed. As a direct participant in a conflict, it is your responsibility to consider the interests of those who are not at the table so they get what they want and need. That means doing a stakeholder analysis to identify those who can influence or be effected by the conflict and its outcome, determining their goals and objectives, the amount of time they are willing to or able to devote to the conflict management process, and their preferences and styles.

Authority and Hierarchy

Hierarchies and authority impact conflict management. Conflicts between people at different levels of hierarchy tend to be more difficult to handle than those between peers. Hierarchies exist between subordinates and superiors and between two people where one has ultimate decision-making authority and the other does not.

The authority to make binding decisions is often held by the managers, clients, or sponsors of the direct participants. For example, in a conflict over the choice of a supplier, the direct participants may have to get approval from above before the choice becomes binding. Know your own limits and the limits of the other parties regarding making binding decisions. This information will help you avoid unnecessary arguments and unrealistic expectations and give you access to the right people at the right time in the process. If your project has been kicked-off well, this information would come out of your stakeholder analysis and responsibility assignments and be stated in your communication plan.

The parties at the lower end of the hierarchy have less power and may be subject to penalties if they displease their superior. They are more likely to encounter inner feelings of fear (worrying about how much they can push an argument without getting the boss angry and resentful), frustration ("no matter what I say, she is just going to do what she wants"), or anger ("What an idiot!").

Knowing this, you can play your role more effectively. As one in authority you can set the other parties at ease, to some degree, by raising the hierarchy issue up front and agreeing on ground rules and techniques that will remove as much of the effect of the hierarchy as possible. For example, you might say "I know I have the power to make this decision unilaterally but I would like to come to the optimal conclusion so I invite you all to raise conflicting ideas and candidly and constructively criticize ideas, including mine". You might go on to recommend making comments anonymously. You might invite the others to suggest ways around the hierarchy issue. We will explore the hierarchy issue again later in the context of cultural differences regarding power.

As one who is not in authority and who is not working for an "enlightened-one," you might raise the issue by suggesting submitting opposing ideas anonymously with a facilitator guiding the process, assuming the situation would allow for it. If there is a chronic issue regarding authority and hierarchies, it can be raised in a project performance review, where it may be depersonalized and analyzed objectively.

However, being in a conflict with your boss or client is never without some degree of emotional response. It is one of those situations in which you must subjectively analyze and be courageous but not foolish. The more you can stick to the facts, be aware of their needs and interests and of their personal issues, the more effectively you can navigate this tricky area.

Organizational Issues

Conflict may occur in various contexts. Cummings, Long, and Lewis (1983) suggested six contexts for conflict in their book, *Managing Communication in Organizations*:

- Intrapersonal—the internal, mental struggle to select from among alternatives
- Interpersonal—differences between individuals
- Intragroup—differences between members of a group pursuing a similar corporate goal
- Intergroup—differences between groups with competing goals
- Intraorganizational—generalized differences in goals or perceptions of various factions within an organization
- Interorganizational—differences between organizations (companies or governments) competing for a similar goal or to advance competing ideologies (Brown, III, n.d.)

Conflict complexity increases significantly as the number of parties, the number of groups, and number of levels crossed increase. For example, a conflict with interpersonal issues (two parties vying for the same promotion or who just don't like one another) in an intergroup (one works for the marketing group and the other for finance) context is very different than the same type of conflict between members of the same team. As we have said, a cost conflict between parties in different organization units (e.g., vendor-client) has a different character than one within the same organization.

Be ready to preemptively avoid unnecessary emotional or relationship conflict caused by context issues. You can bring in outside facilitators, agree to sound escalation approaches, and openly discuss legal issues related to interorganizational conflicts, etc., that will affect the group's ability to come to an optimal resolution.

In general, there is a greater need for formality when conflicts cut across groups and even more so when they cut across organizations.

Address chronic issues as part of performance evaluation and review and seek behavioral change. For example, if there are chronic disputes between functional group managers and project managers over schedules, then addressing the estimating process and multi-project management approach may eliminate or reduce the frequency of disputes. Similarly, conflicts between design groups and manufacturing or service groups may be positively affected by including these groups in early design and requirements definition sessions.

With interorganizational conflicts we have a need to be aware of legal issues, proprietary property, profit vs. cost conflict, etc. As with intergroup conflicts, assess the need for outside help and make sure you have a healthy process.

Good contracts (a subject for another book) make for fewer conflicts because they set the stage for realistic expectations and provide guidance on how to proceed. Contracts result from conflict resolutions and from collaborative efforts to minimize conflict later or make it as easy as possible to resolve. Use your understanding of the types of conflict that typically occur to predict and resolve as many as you can before the work starts; make the solutions part of the contract. In addition, consider the conflict management process itself and include appropriate agreements about it in your contracts. Remember, even when working within a single organization informal or non-legally binding contracts exist, explicitly or tacitly.

Personalities and Preferences

In addition to knowing the authority of the participants and where they are in the organization, it is quite useful to know something about their personalities. What are their thinking, conflict management, and communication styles? For example, if you are facing a conflict with someone who is your superior, it is useful to have a sense of the degree to which that person relies on the authority of his or her position when in conflict and how much he or she values your ability to confront and argue your points convincingly. See the chapter on conflict styles for more on this topic.

What are their backgrounds (professionally and personally)? Know what language they speak and what makes them comfortable and uncomfortable. See the sections on Diversity and Facilitating Rapport for information on these topics.

Know what motivates them. See the section on Cognitive Analysis for details on this topic.

Some of the information about the stakeholders comes to light as you engage the other parties. Some of it can be determined beforehand by doing research and engaging people who have worked with the other parties. Depending on the situation, you may have more or less time to prepare and get to know the other parties. When there is little time to prepare, you rely on your intuition and on your ability to operate effectively in the moment. The ability to operate in the moment is discussed further in the sections on Emotional Intelligence and Mindfulness.

Chapter Summary

Conflicts are inevitable in projects. Avoiding unnecessary conflicts and resolving the rest at the right time and in the right way is critical to project success. This can be achieved by the following:

- Raising issues and forcing conflict at the right places in project life;
- Pre-empting challenges like cross-organizational boundaries and hierarchies by airing them before they emerge and finding effective ways to moderate their effects;

- Improving the way you schedule, estimate, define requirements, choose designs, manage change and issues, procure products and services, plan and communicate and the other things that cause or influence conflicts; and
- Analyzing your conflicts to see if there are patterns and, if there are, seeking out and working on the causes to find ways to avoid unnecessary conflicts and make resolutions easier and more effective.

Conflicts occur across project life. It is likely that they will be more intense and difficult to address if they do not occur at the right time,

Conflicts occur between stakeholders who may or may not be on the same team, group, or organization. Hierarchies and organizational alignment affect the way people behave in conflicts.

The common types of conflicts that occur in projects are

- Schedule conflicts
- Priorities conflicts
- Resource conflicts
- Technical conflicts
- Administrative procedures conflicts
- Personality conflicts
- Cost conflicts
- Performance conflicts
- Supplier selection conflicts

These include conflicts about designs, methods, who gets what resources when, when things will be delivered, how they will be tested, where people sit, how they dress, who reports to who and how they do it, who decides what, what vendor to hire, etc.

Now that we have a sense of what conflicts in projects are like and, in the abstract, what we can do about them. We will turn our attention to conflict management as a process and the foundation concepts that underlie it. Then we will address the nature and anatomy of a conflict before identifying and discussing people related issues and techniques.

Chapter 3

Foundation Concepts

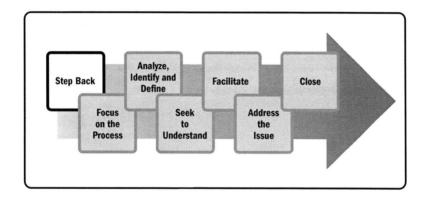

Chapter Overview

Underlying the conflict management approach in this book are five key foundation concepts (Figure 3-1).

This chapter describes each of the key conflict management foundation concepts. They will be integrated in the process in subsequent chapters. Having a sense of these concepts as a backdrop for the application of the techniques, methods, and ideas that make up our approach to conflict management better enables you to excel at it.

As we discuss objectivity, we will explore the first, and arguably the most important, step in the conflict management process—stepping back.

Practicality

Conflicts are inevitable. In projects we are driven by practicality—what will reduce the number of unnecessary and damaging conflicts and what will make for optimal solutions and healthy long-term relationships, while optimizing time and effort and recognizing the needs and capabilities of the participants?

Many disputes and conflicts must be resolved in the short term, quickly and easily, for practical purposes. This leads to a choice of conflict resolution approach

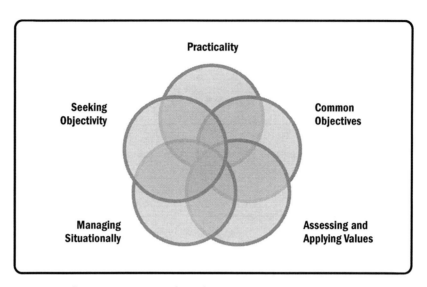

Figure 3.1: Key conflict management foundation concepts

(consensus—which generally takes a long time, vs. authority, majority, or plurality—all of which take less time and effort). Choice of approach in turn affects buy-in and the quality of the resolution.

Perhaps the most important practical reality is that conflict is people centric. No people; no conflict. We, people, are as alike and as different as snowflakes are from one another with varying degrees of emotional intelligence, values, intellectual intelligence, knowledge, experience, thinking orientations, cultural norms, perceptions, needs, and so forth. Each party to the conflict is managing himself or herself and their relationships with the others while a project manager may be managing the conflict as a whole. Everyone needs to be a knowledgeable, emotionally intelligent conflict manager . Unfortunately, everyone is not. The chapter on the People Side of Conflict Management and Facilitating Rapport will explore these issues in greater depth.

Common Overriding Objectives

Objectives drive both projects and conflicts. People who disagree and who share an interest in achieving common objectives are more likely to resolve their conflicts amicably. For example, if a project manager and a functional manager in charge of one of the organizations that provide people and services to the project share an interest in making the organization they work for as profitable as possible they are more likely to work together to resolve or avoid conflicts over priorities for the assignment of resources. The more the parties can find a common overriding objective, the greater the possibility that they can reach win-win outcomes even when one party "wins" something and another "loses" something.

Cooperation and collaboration among conflicting parties concentrating on a common problem transforms conflict into something that not only results in optimal resolutions but also focuses consciously on building healthy relationships to eliminate unnecessary and dysfunctional conflicts and make the remaining ones easier to manage. The most obvious common objectives in project work are the success of the project and the success of the organization.

Values

Though there are similarities, values are different from objectives. Common objectives help people to focus their energy at something besides one another. Common values, or at least values that are clearly known, help people work together with less effort. If you know that an overriding value of another party is to win at all cost, it helps you to more easily predict his or her behavior. If you know he or she values long-term relationships over quick wins, you are more likely to trust him or her.

Values are what people find significant, important, or worthwhile. A value system is an enduring set of beliefs ranked in terms of their relative importance about the most effective way of behaving. The following section explores values in more depth.

Positive Values and Their Effect

The list of positive values that effect conflict management is a long one. It includes honesty, candor, and trustworthiness that are supported by transparency and accountability; service orientation, emotional intelligence, collaboration, non-harming, respect for diversity, empathy (which implies kindness and compassion); perseverance and the motivation to win, objectivity, precision, practicality, profitability and organizational success. Table 3-1 recaps and describes core values.

Clearly articulated values, particularly if they are supported by senior management, make dysfunctional behavior obvious and when such behavior is brought to light, it is hard for even the most die-hard politicos to continue it. Why do clearly articulated values have this positive effect? They do because the combination of peer pressure and pressure from above make it less likely that individuals will act in selfish, divisive, and dishonest ways. By addressing them early in project life and/or as a part of an organization-wide education program, positive values can be made an integral part of performance.

Here are examples of conflicts that are rooted in values:

- In a global project in a large financial institution, members of two departments fought about who would be in charge—the performance group (IT applications development) or the project management group. The values of collaboration and organizational success were not among their priorities. They were more interested in protecting their perceived autonomy and authority than in

Table 3.1: Values for Creating an Optimal Performance Environment

Value	Supporting Values
Trustworthiness	Honesty, candor, reliability, transparency and accountability, service orientation, open-mindedness, kindness
Collaboration	Emotional intelligence, non-harming, respect for diversity, empathy, trustworthiness, kindness and compassion, effective communication
Perseverance	Motivation to succeed, self-confidence
Open-mindedness	Objectivity, practicality, humility, respect for others
Organizational success	Profitability, motivation to succeed, loyalty, practicality
Quality results	Precision, accuracy, clearly defined and weighted criteria,
Stakeholder satisfaction	Quality results, trustworthiness, organizational success, timeliness
Clear, candid communications	Objectivity, emotional intelligence, open-mindedness, respect for diversity, practicality
Adaptability	Practicality, emotional intelligence, resilience

getting a rather large complex expensive and mission critical project done. Note that this is not a vacuum of values, there are values at play, and they are just ones that conflict with what is best for the project and organization.

- A sales team's value of winning contracts was prioritized over the values of honesty and rationality.
- Conflicts over schedule and budget compliance arose when managers valued pleasing their superiors in the same way the sales people valued winning contracts. They promised to deliver anything their superiors wanted regardless of the effect on their subordinates.
- Conflict between manager and performer over a performance review in which the manager gave a subordinate a poor rating because the person was often late in delivering results or came in with estimates that were perceived as inflated. The manager highly valued timeliness and cost while the performer highly valued product quality and quality of life.

These conflicts of values resulted in regular disputes about role and responsibility issues, who were to blame for late and over budget projects and low profit margins, etc. Had the underlying values of collaboration and organizational benefits, autonomy and power, quality and profitability, etc. been addressed early on, for example, by discussing them or by having them reflected in performance measurement and reward systems, unnecessary conflicts could have been be avoided or made far easier to handle.

Many organizations and individuals alike never really explore their values. Defining, agreeing to, and acting on values are part of establishing a healthy conflict management culture. It takes the time and effort to break through resistance to addressing "philosophy" and the "soft side" of behavior.

We will see later how cognitive analysis with its exploration of the interests that motivate conflicting parties allows you to cut through conflict and arrive at win-win resolutions. However, the cognitive approach does not necessarily address higher-level values, such as the ones in Table 3-1.

You can use these to start a discussion on values and how you will integrate them into the project. You can prompt participants to address any conflicts or issues they have in working with these values. If your organization has a published values statement use it to start the discussion about applying those values to the project at hand.

Adaptability and Situational Management

Our conflict management approach recognizes the need for adaptability in the face of complex interpersonal relationships within complex projects and organizations.

Managing conflict successfully requires that you understand the causes of the conflict, the influence of external factors, the effect of when in the life of the project the conflict occurs, and the state of mind of the people concerned, among other factors. Analyzing the conflict using the taxonomy introduced in the chapters on "Conflict in Projects and Analysis: The Nature of Conflict" and having a sense of the players and their nature using the models in the sections on "Seeking to Understand and The People Side of Conflict Management" will provide the information required to make the situationally appropriate choices of the right tools and techniques.

Adaptability implies the ability to size up a situation in real-time and apply the right words and actions. It implies resilience or the ability to cope with stress and adversity, particularly when faced with change and uncertainty.

Objectivity: Open-mindedness

Open-mindedness is the next of our basic principles. It is the "willingness to consider new and different ideas" (Open-minded, n.d.). It is dispassionately assessing whatever is occurring; questioning all beliefs and assumptions; open to change. Open-mindedness is based on objectivity and on both knowledge of facts, opinions, and assumptions and knowledge of what drives your behavior and the behavior of the other parties. Open-mindedness encourages you to moderate passionate advocacy for your point of view with a healthy degree of objectivity. Mindfulness is a critical element in being open-minded and objective.

It is likely that both in the context of projects and in the broader context of life that we have all succumbed to thinking that we were completely right and justified about something. We were convinced but later we found out that we were misguided. How many of your conflicts are rooted in differences of opinion in which the parties fail to explore the validity of their opinion? They debate convinced that their position is right and fail to modify their views in light of facts and their opponents' logical arguments. When this happens, the result is often an inability to reach resolution without escalating or, worse, a sub-optimal resolution with bad feelings about the other person's obstinacy and lack of flexibility. We will look more deeply into open-mindedness in the following sections.

Multiple Perspectives and the Power of Conflict

The need for open-mindedness is founded on the idea that an individual's view of a complex issue is limited and distorted by personality, cultural conditioning, and other factors, including the person's mood. Taking multiple perspectives makes it more likely to reach an objective understanding of the issue.

The story of the Blind Men and the Elephant is a parable that makes this point.

> "Once upon a time, there was a village populated entirely by blind people. The villagers had heard that an elephant was going to be passing through their vicinity. These people had never encountered an elephant before, so the villagers sent out a small delegation to bring back a report.
>
> The delegation members experienced the beast using their sense of touch. When they returned to the village, everyone was gathered in the village center to learn about the elephant.
>
> The first delegate said, "An elephant is like a snake." He was immediately interrupted by another person who said, "That's ridiculous. An elephant is like a tree trunk." Another shouted, "No, an elephant is like a rope with a tuft at the end." And someone else said, "No, an elephant is like a wall."
>
> Soon, all of the delegation members were arguing. Voices raised. Epithets and insults flying.
>
> Most of the villagers became frustrated and left. Some people, liking a good argument, stayed to listen. Some began to create logical constructs based on what they had heard, adding a few statements of their own based on their opinions. "An elephant should be this," or "logically an elephant would be that," they said.
>
> Others knew that if their brother-in-law said that an elephant was one thing, it couldn't possibly be the case—and they jumped in. *What* was right didn't matter to them, just *who* was right.
>
> In the end—there is no end to this story. The argument continues to this day. The elephant is replaced by a complex product design, the contents of a meeting, or the cause of a problem. This is what happens when people close-mindedly debate instead of engaging in dialogue with one another" Pitagorsky, 2000).

"Imagine if one of the delegation members had said "Interesting that we can have such diverse impressions of the elephant." And then followed up with, "Why don't we spend some time exploring how we might explain and even reconcile the differences." It wouldn't be much of a parable, but chances are the villagers would have been a lot more likely to get an accurate sense of the nature of the elephant. It would have also avoided all the yelling, cursing and insulting" (Pitagorsky, 2001).

Both-and vs. Either-or Thinking

Both-and thinking (i.e., seemingly exclusive positions seen as being compatible) is an important means to open-mindedness. In my experience and based on feedback from people in hundreds of courses and consulting situations, many conflicts are fueled by *either-or* thinking: "It has to be this way and not that way. If the elephant is a wall then it can't be a tree."

Sometimes it is true that things must be one-way or another. However, more often, when it comes to conflicts over plans, designs, ideas, and estimates, there are many possible right answers and there is the paradox that seemingly mutually exclusive ideas can coexist.

"A hybrid, combined approach is really the only approach that makes any sense. In religion many people worship only one god, but in process management we should all be pantheists." Tom Davenport (2008).

Either-or thinking is a sure way to get to poor decisions and divisiveness. Tom Davenport's quote refers to the use of Six Sigma but applies in many contexts including project management, design engineering, strategic planning, marketing, and management in general. When we try to squeeze a complex problem into a preset methodology or style, we invariably run into trouble.

Step Back - Get Centered

Stepping back is a key to success in managing conflict. It is the first step in the process of managing conflict, which is presented, in the Chapter 3. We discuss it here under foundation concepts because it is the primary means to cultivating the objectivity needed to take a responsive, effective conflict management approach. What does it mean to step back? It means to change perspective; to separate from your ideas, beliefs, and emotions and to view things objectively.

It has been said that project managers are driven by action and outcomes. A colleague advised that they would not appreciate or have empathy for the idea behind stepping back to take a breath and calmly assess the situation.

I think this attitude shows a serious misunderstanding of what effective project management is all about. Of course, we want action and outcomes, but we recognize that to get them in the most optimal way we must plan. To do so we must step back and assess our circumstances, our stakeholders, the project's objectives, the capacity and availability of resources, risks, and more. To just dive in and take action is a sure way to failure.

We apply the same principle to conflict management. A conflict can be seen as a mini project (we seek to achieve an objective within finite time and cost constraints), so there is need to step back, assess, and plan before we get into the negotiation and debate that addresses the content.

So, take a breath, sense your body, and relax. Then you are ready to assess the situation and act, or not. Be proactive; not reactive.

> Try it now. Step back from the reading. Follow your breath and just feel your body for a minute. Then come back to the reading. Does it change your attitude or your concentration?

Be Responsive Rather Than Reactive

Self-management is the ability to act in a situationally appropriate, way even in the face of strong personal emotions or conditioned habits, tendencies, and beliefs. Why is this important? It is important because if you simply act out your emotions or do what "comes naturally," you are likely to transform content conflict into relationship conflict and that will make achieving your goals more difficult. It is very practical to control yourself so that you can be more effective in interpersonal relationships. Interpersonal relationships are at the heart of conflict management.

While as a project manager you are driven by action and outcomes, it is to your benefit to stop and reflect before you act. It will likely make your outcomes more to your liking.

Conflict often brings on emotions. For example, you come up with a great idea, present it, and are met with "There's got to be a better way." Or. you come to the table with a well thought out estimate of how long it will take to complete a project and the boss or client says, "Too much time you have to get it done by _____, no matter what."

If your initial response is a sense of frustration, anger, or fear, you are normal. If you act out of those emotions, you may still be normal but, you are likely to fail to reach an optimum resolution and are likely to damage relationships.

So, what to do?

Take a Breath and Get Centered

Take a step back and remind yourself that you are *not* your idea or your estimate. Remember that you are involved in an activity (whether a project, process, or personal relationship) that is bigger than your conflict.

Get *centered*. Take a breath, feel your body, relax. Remind yourself that you are *not* your position, idea, or estimate. Then assess the situation and choose your response. Be proactive, not reactive. The ability to respond rather than react is a critical success factor in conflict management.

Ready for anything

The parable of the Fighting Cock sets out the idea that it is only when we are non-reactive that we are ready for anything and ready to win.

The Fighting Cock by Chuang Tzu

Chi Hsing Tzu was a king's trainer of fighting cocks.
He was training a fine bird.
The king kept asking
if the bird was ready for combat.

"Not yet", said the trainer.
"He is full of fire.
He is ready to pick a fight
with every other bird.
He is vain and confident
of his own strength."

After ten days he answered again,
"Not yet. He flares up
when he hears another bird crow."

After ten more days,
"Not yet. He still gets that angry look
and ruffles his feathers."

Again ten days.
The trainer said,
"Now he is nearly ready.
When another bird crows,
his eyes don't even flicker.
He stands immobile like a block of wood.
He is a mature fighter.
Other birds will take one look at him and run."[1]

---

[1] http://www.messagefrommasters.com/Stories/chuangtzu/Fighting_Cock. htm

Being Centered

What does it mean to step back and get centered? To step back is to change perspective. It is to separate yourself from your ideas, beliefs, and emotions and to view things objectively.

Being centered is being calm in the rush of the moment's events, including your thoughts. Being centered is being in touch with the sense of self that is not bothered by preferences, passion, fear, anger, pleasure or pain. It doesn't mean that you don't experience all of these. It means you experience them without having to react to them. They don't drive your behavior; you choose your behavior.

When you are centered and have a clear mind, then you are ready to manage conflict. You are ready for anything.

Mindfulness

So, how do you get centered? One method is cultivating mindfulness so that you can quickly see when you are getting off center and bring yourself back before you act inappropriately or lose your concentration and focus.

Mindfulness is objective awareness of one's thoughts and feelings. It is the fundamental enabler of self-awareness, self-management, and relationship management. To cultivate emotional intelligence, cultivate mindfulness. Mindfulness will allow you to sense your emotions before they take over and drive your behavior.

If you choose to be responsive rather than reactive, cultivating mindfulness of your thoughts is necessary. The quote from the Dharmapada tells us why.

Watching Your Thoughts and Feelings

The thought manifests as the word
The word manifests as the deed
The deed develops into habit and
And habit hardens into character,
So watch the thought and its ways with care
and let it spring from love,
Born out of concern for all beings. . .
As the shadow follows the body'
as we think, so we become.

Buddha

Mindfulness Meditation

How can you watch your thoughts and their ways with care? One way is to practice mindfulness or insight meditation. It is quite simple:

> Sit or stand comfortably erect;
> Choose a point of reference—for example, your breath or the sensations of your body;
> Observe it along with any thoughts, feelings, sounds, sights, or smells that might arise;

When you realize that you have become distracted, return to your point of reference; and
Continue.

Do this formally for anywhere from five minutes to an hour a day in a quiet, comfortable place. Over time, mindfulness and concentration will increase. You will "space-out" less. You will be more able to see emotions arising, before they erupt into reactive behavior. Stress relief is a welcome side effect; you will become calmer. You will find it increasingly easy to get centered. Being mindfully centered becomes natural.

If formal practice isn't for you, practice informally. Make your reference point a sense of attentiveness, the body, or the breath. Note your breath every occasionally to see whether you are distracted or reactive. If you are, focus on your breath and body for a moment and then reengage. With practice, this becomes completely integrated into your normal behavior. You will "lose it" less frequently and for shorter periods.

Chapter Summary

In this chapter, we have identified and described five foundation concepts:

- Practicality;
- Common overriding objectives;
- Values and their effect on conflict management;
- Adaptability and situational management; and
- Stepping back to achieve objectivity and open-mindedness using mindfulness meditation.

These are integrated into our approach. They provide a solid base for addressing conflict in a way that makes sense in the complex realm of projects in organizations and that leads to the fulfillment of the goals of effective resolutions, healthy relationships, personal growth, and ongoing improvement in the management of conflict

Chapter 4

Process

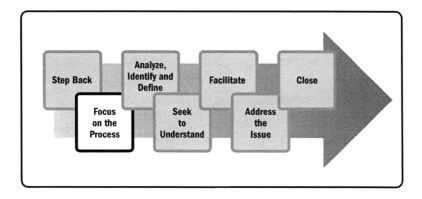

<u>All</u> results arise out of sets of steps or actions in a process.

Nothing appears spontaneously. Everything is caused by something.

To find out how something came about, study the causes and conditions (the process and its environment) that brought it about. To create a particular outcome, identify the causes and conditions that are likely to bring it about and engineer a process to do it.

Remember that when working with people and organizations there is complexity and uncertainty. The processes are non-linear; there are cycles and feedback loops with multiple levels of dependencies and continuously changing conditions.

Chapter Overview

This chapter explores conflict management as a process and describes a stepwise approach that incorporates the foundation concepts of practicality, common objectives, values, situational management, and objectivity.

When we look at conflict management within the project management process, it fits within communication management.

Consider Process Complexity

Conflicts involve people working in and around projects. Because people, projects, and their environments are complex, to decide on how best to address your situation you must see the big picture as well as its parts (the people, organizations, facts, facilities, tools, techniques, etc.) and the relationships among them.

Consider the interplay among multiple factors, such as the need for speed and a good decision, the nature of the players, their relationships and environment, present and future impacts, and others. Think about your decision's impact "downstream" on the activities and people who will be affected. Look "upstream" to the causes and conditions that led to the current situation to make sure you have identified the true causes, not just the immediate spark, of your conflict and think about any unintended consequences of possible solutions.

Consider the delay between action and reaction and the uncertainty that arises from complex relationships in which a person's mood or external influences such as culture and change in market conditions can change the way people respond to the same stimulus.

Considering these factors will help you predict how your actions are likely to influence the environment and how the environment is likely to influence you. Note the word "likely." Given the complex nature of the conflict management process and the organizations we live and work in, there is no way to completely determine the outcome of a particular action with 100 percent accuracy. Adaptability is essential.

We will explore complexity and the attributes of conflicts in more depth in the next chapter.

Types of Processes

To have a true sense of conflict management as a process, it is important to see how the interplay between internal and external processes affects performance.

External and Internal Processes

Any process that involves the interplay among people or people and machines is an external process. In external processes there are discernible behaviors, events, and flows of information between the people or machines.

Internal processes occur within an individual. For example, they are the mental events (thoughts, feelings, and moods) that are set off by a stimulus (initiating event). We care about them because they emerge as behavior that influences the external processes that, in our case, affect the way people relate to one another when in conflict.

Imagine a dispute about whether to immediately get started with the work or to step back and plan first.

- Fred says to Charlie, "You must be either stupid or crazy to think that." Charlie becomes angry, says something like "Who the—are you to tell me I'm stupid?" and a spiraling angry argument between the two results.
- It seems as if Fred's words caused the argument. In fact, it was each party's internal process that caused it. Internal processes occur very quickly (tenths to hundredths of a second) and are conditioned by a combination of psychological and physiological factors that operate on one another. Mental models, moods, emotional intelligence, and degrees of mindfulness, among other factors influence the process.
- Charlie hears Fred's words, interprets them, evaluates the interpretation, reacts to the interpretation, formulates a response, and responds. Fred does the same.

One doesn't have to be a psychologist or neuroscientist to understand that it is Charlie's internal process, as opposed to Fred's words (the initiating event), that creates the result. Consider that the same words under different conditions can lead to alternative results. Charlie could have seen his internal reaction, taken a breath (or ten), and simply said with a smile, "Well Fred, tell me why you think I am crazy?" Then there is a dialogue instead of an angry argument.

The process steps, not the event, cause the result. For example, pressing a doorbell is an event. It initiates a process including transmission of electricity through a wire to ring the bell. You can change the connection between the doorbell button and the bell; cut it, or rewire it to play a tune instead of going ding-dong.

Defined and Undefined Processes

> "If you can't describe what you are doing as a process, you don't know what you are doing."—Dr. W. Edwards Deming (http://www.quotes.net/quote/8537)

Undefined processes are not articulated or documented. An undefined process cannot be evaluated and improved.

Every process can be defined. In some organizations some processes (for example, specific technical procedures) must be defined in great detail and followed to the letter for safe and effective results. Other processes, like conflict management, are so complex and subject to changing conditions that a detailed rigidly adhered to process definition is at least as ineffective as no definition at all.

Strike a right balance by identifying the level of detail required. The definition of the conflict management process should identify major activities and techniques and following the principle of situational management, to give the practitioner the responsibility to adapt the process to current conditions. The framework later in this chapter can be used as a starting point for your process definition.

Process Certainty and Uncertainty

Processes, whether defined or not, may have predictable results that are the same each time the process is performed. The output is 100 percent determined by the input. Push the button and the bell rings.

Other processes, including conflict management, involve chance or probability. The result is determined by both the process and by events that influence the outcomes of process steps. Process controls minimize the effects of uncertainty. Variations can be corrected to a predicted result or the prediction can be changed in response to outside influences.

As we saw in the case of Fred and Charlie, if in a dispute one of the parties uses words like "stupid or crazy", or even looks at the other the wrong way, the outcome depends on the 'receiving' party's frame of mind and his level of emotional intelligence. If he is relatively competent, he will take no effect, realizing that the poor choice of words need not derail the process. On the other hand, he could react and help the conflict spiral out of control.

However, in less predictable processes, over multiple interactions, there is greater predictability. If the parties share a history of working out their differences, even though they may have some short-term spats it is relatively predictable that the overall outcome will be positive. If on the other hand, they have a history of poorly handled conflicts and animosity is growing among the parties, a negative outcome is relatively predictable, unless the parties change their process.

Engineer the Process

The idea that the parties can change their process is an important one. It is what leads us into process engineering. We want to engineer or refine the conflict management process to make it more predictable.

The optimal conflict management process leaves plenty of room for creative adaptation, using a variety of techniques within a framework. An over-engineered process is less likely to be a true reflection of the real world; under-engineering opens up too much unnecessary uncertainty. Creative adaptation or situational management keeps the process on target to achieve the desired outcome.

In a competitive sport, there are structures—rules, physical specifications for field layout, etc.– that the competing parties agree to and follow because if they do not they will be penalized or ejected from the game. There are referees or umpires with the power to make binding decisions.

To what degree does your situation need a clearly defined and mutually understood process that includes the definition of the authority of the ultimate decision makers?

Generally, less formality is needed when the participants are on the same team, the issue is not critical or complex, and the parties have maturity in conflict management and emotional intelligence. However, when dealing with critical and complex situations, or when the parties have different goals (for example, vendors vying for a contract, or clients vying for scarce resources) more formality is needed. Consider how a formal procurement process at least attempts to minimize emotion-based conflict and promote an even playing field with rules that set a structure that benefits the buyer and sellers.

Consider the metaphor of tuning an instrument. Make the strings too tight, and they will break as you are playing; if they are not tight enough, you won't get the sound you want. In managing conflict, make the process resilient and leave it open for interpretation and moment to moment decision making by the players while at the same time including sufficient rigor and discipline to avoid unnecessary problems and promote a desired end result.

Process Definition Unifies the Conflicting Parties

The definition of the conflict management process can occur at the beginning of a project as part of kicking off the project, as part of organizational planning and behavioral skills training or it can occur at the onset, or at any time, during a conflict.

Ideally, the parties dynamically work together to define or tailor their process, assess its practicality, agree upon, sustain and continuously refine their approach. It is an opportunity to create a subtle shift from antagonistic disputants to members of a team who join forces to confront the conflict as opposed to one another.

Of course, there may be conflicts about the way to address the conflict, and these can take a good deal of effort to resolve. In the negotiations to end the Vietnam War, there was a lengthy dispute over the shape of the negotiators' table. However, these process disputes are easier to address than the core conflict itself. If they are not addressed and reconciled, they will come up and influence the core conflict. The focus on process increases the probability that the right techniques will be used, making an optimal outcome more likely. The parties will better understand one another as they address these peripheral issues.

The Conflict Management Process

To engineer the conflict management process, analyze your situation thoroughly. Consider the stakeholders and their roles and responsibilities, the logistics, and the most appropriate techniques for your situation given the need for speed, the skill levels of the participants, the available technology, etc.

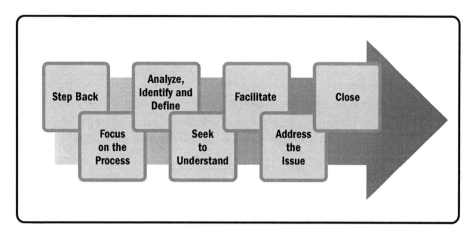

Figure 4.1: The conflict management process

When you have a sense of the steps, the documentation needs, logistics, and timings make them part of your project communication plan. Define the process with the degrees of detail and documentation that fit the situation's needs. Be ready to adapt your plan to the situation as things change, and they will change. The communication plan is discussed further later in this chapter.

The steps in our conflict management process framework are shown in Figure 4-1.

The overlapping blocks in Figure 4-1 are meant to show that the process is not fully linear. While there is a logical sequence, the steps overlap and reinforce one another.

Let's briefly describe each step. This chapter addresses the second step, the first step was covered in the preceding chapter, and subsequent chapters address the remaining steps.

Stepping back promotes objectivity. It is applied throughout the process, not just at the start. Pause and think before you react. At least for a moment, detach from your emotions and position and become an objective witness. Open your mind to the possibility that you may be wrong or that you can adjust your position to satisfy your needs while also working to satisfy the needs of the others. Process management, analysis, and seeking to understand are all means for stepping back and seeing the conflict as an object to be addressed jointly by the participants for mutual benefit.

Focusing on and defining the process is best done early in project life, but the process must be revisited to ensure that it continues to be the right one for each situation. Join with the other parties to face the conflict by focusing on the process.

Analysis results in the information needed to decide how you will manage the conflict. Analyzing seeks to understand the nature of the conflict at hand. Like focusing on the process, it also involves stepping back to objectify the conflict and minimize emotionality and reactivity. While it is addressed most intensively early in the life of a conflict, it is a continuous process as the conflict is handled and more information emerges.

Seeking to understand oneself and others sets a stage for the development of rapport making it easier to get to know and understand the other parties and their tendencies, motivations, values, and positions. It is an extension of the analysis that focuses on the people as opposed to the conflict. It can be done as a joint effort or individually by the parties.

Facilitating rapport sets the stage for effectively addressing the content. It enables candid communications. This step may, as with the others, begin early in the life of both the project and the conflict situation, but it is continued throughout conflict life as greater insight into the nature of the participants and their motivations, thinking styles, and values emerge during interactions.

Addressing the issue, every other part of the process is enabling the use of the right tools and techniques, including facilitation and communication to get to closure.

Closure addresses agreement, including the agreement to disagree, to end a conflict and promote action on the decisions made. It addresses improvement into the future based on a review of the experience.

This process is a framework, not a cookbook. As you define your process, make it an integral part of your project's communication plan. If you don't have a communication plan, make one. It will save you from easily avoidable conflicts and make the unavoidable ones far easier to handle. If you can, develop communication plans at an enterprise or organizational level and apply them flexibly in projects.

The Communications Plan

Conflict management is essentially a communication process in which the parties exchange facts and opinions to address their issues. Effective communication can avoid unnecessary conflict by eliminating miscommunication. Miscommunication is a prime cause of conflict, it leads to the perception of differences that don't exist, or perceptions that make simple disputes difficult to resolve.

As many project managers know, a project communications plan outlines

- who will communicate with whom,
- about what,
- where,
- when, and
- how they will do it.

It addresses the management of information about the project's current state and projected future and includes an annotated list of stakeholders. It defines the way people will communicate about different issues (*conflicts*, issues, changes, the results of decisions, status, etc.), when scheduled communications and event driven communications are done, and what technology will be used. It might define terminology, tone, and the appropriate protocols for different situations.

The communication plan is the ideal place for the definition of the conflict management process. For example, the communications plan defines an escalation process and protocols for how and when to escalate different kinds of conflicts. The escalation process identifies "time frames and the management chain (names) for escalation of issues that cannot be resolved at lower staff levels" (Project Management Institute, 2008, p. 257). The communication plan defines who has what levels of authority to resolve different types of conflicts. We will address escalation in the Chapter 10, "Closure."

Other parts of the communications plan that directly address conflict management issues are these:

- Information language, format, content and level of detail;
- People responsible for communicating and for authorizing the release of confidential information;
- Methods and technologies for conveying information and addressing issues; and
- Information flow diagrams with authorization sequences (Project Management Institute, 2008).

Logistics

Logistics are also part of the communications plan. Conflicts take place within a physical environment and the physical environment has an impact on the way conflict is managed.

Using our sports analogy, imagine playing American football on a field made for the kind of football Americans call soccer. A conflict has a field within which it takes place.

In projects, the parties may be in the same physical office or on different continents. Virtual environments are increasingly common, even in small- to mid-sized organizations, as people work from home, transportation becomes increasingly expensive and sources of goods and services become more geographically dispersed.

As you plan to address conflicts, consider the following:

- Location—Is it neutral or does it give one party advantage? Is it comfortable? Does it set a tone that reflects the kind of relationship desired among the parties? What works best a coffee shop, park bench, outdoors in a garden, in a formal conference room, in someone's cubicle?

- The shape of the table—If you will be at a table then do you want the parties to be in a circle or around the sides of a rectangle? Do you want members of the sides of a conflict to be on opposite sides or interspersed? How close will people be to one another? What will be between them? Will they have room for materials? Will support people be at the table or seated behind the principal they are supporting?
- Privacy—Will participants feel comfortable to be candid? Will there be interruptions? Will the proceedings be recorded?
- Technology—what will be needed to support communication and decision making? Will people be familiar with the technology and the implications of its use? Consider telephone, text messaging, email, blogs, wikis, on-line discussion groups, web meetings, and video conferencing.

Logistics are heavily influenced by the degree to which a conflict is to be handled synchronously (with all the parties present either physically or virtually at the same time) or not.

Synchronous Communications

Synchronous communication takes place with the parties present at the same time. They may or may not be collocated. In general, it is quicker and usually easier to address conflicts via synchronous communication and when people are co-located (though inexpensive video conferencing is making co-location less of an issue).

When faced with a minor dispute, you can operate almost anywhere, under any conditions. In a healthy team made up of members who are comfortable with one another, conflicts over issues like task estimates, approaches to task performance, and others that require short-term resolutions can be addressed and resolved over any one of the parties' desks, in a conference room, over the coffee maker in the common room, in a phone call, at a chance meeting in the hall or via e-mail or an online discussion group.

If the issue is more complex and likely to have long-range impact, or where one or more parties are emotionally attached to their positions, choose a neutral ground - perhaps a conference room, a coffee shop, or the office of a neutral party. If logistical conditions make physical co-location, impossible video conferencing or web conferencing can work fine, assuming the meetings are appropriately facilitated.

If a means for presenting information, playing "what if games" after modeling the problem and its environment, and/or taking notes are required then a location that has tools like a flip chart, white board, computer, overhead projector, or a monitor big enough to allow everyone to see what is going on and how the conflict issue is unfolding. You might have technology that enables anonymous polling, diagramming, weights, and scores analysis or other group facilitation and problem-solving/decision-making techniques. These are particularly useful in complex conflicts—if you know how to use them.

As geographically dispersed groups become more and more the norm, make virtual communications as effective as possible. This means not only getting used to the technology but also making better use of intuition and interpersonal skills in the absence of face-to-face, co-located communication.

Asynchronous Communications

Asynchronous communications are among people who are not present at the same time. Some conflicts can be nicely managed under such conditions. Again, it depends on factors like the complexity and criticality of the subject and the skills and relationships among the parties. Asynchronous communication relies on technology (e-mail, social networks, wikis, etc.). The parties must communicate well in writing and commit to timely response.

Imagine a conflict between colleagues regarding which of two color schemes to use for an ad campaign. Their schedules do not allow them to meet face-to-face or even to set a remote meeting that would give them the time to work things out. So they use e-mail to send sample layouts and discuss the pros and cons of each option. It might take a bit longer than it would if they could get an hour or two to meet together but they could reach an amicable and optimal agreement asynchronously.

A side benefit of asynchronous conflict management is that it leaves documentation and enables the parties to escalate more easily if necessary. Another benefit is that it helps to avoid emotionality because people have more time to reflect before they say or do something. This assumes that the parties can write well enough to avoid unintended insults and to convey moods and attitudes in a way that does not stir up unproductive emotional responses.

Also, the reflection needed for writing responses generally leads to greater clarity and precision.

Often, asynchronous communication may set things up for a brief synchronous meeting that would resolve issues that could not be resolved asynchronously.

Chapter Summary—Process

Everything that occurs is the result of a process—a set of steps or actions and events occurring under environmental conditions. Internal processes occur within individuals and influence external behavior. External processes are among people and machines, they can be observed objectively. Conflict management is an external process that is heavily influenced by the participants' internal processes.

Conflict management is a process that does not have definitive predictable outcomes each time it is performed. The variables that make conflict situations unpredictable center on the way the people involved behave and react to one another's behavior. Behavior is influenced by factors as diverse as cultural conditioning, mood, personality, stress, regulatory requirements, and the perceived value and impact of the outcome, among others.

Defining the conflict management process, with its appropriate formality and tools, as part of the communications plan, adds value because it provides a framework that can help the participants avoid reactive behavior and enables consistency and continuous improvement over time. It makes it possible to more easily identify and address chronic problems in conflict management.

The factors that influence the degree of formality and the tools needed are conflict criticality, complexity, the nature of the relationships among the parties, and their degree of healthy conflict management sophistication and emotional intelligence.

The remaining chapters address the action taken in the steps we have identified in the conflict management process framework.

Chapter 5

Analysis: The Nature of a Conflict

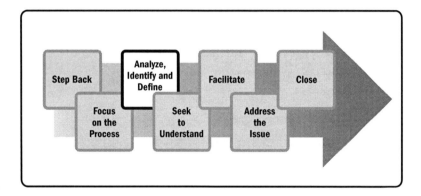

Chapter Overview

In the previous chapters, we explored conflict management as a process and stepping back as a foundation concept. These represent the first two steps in the conflict management process. Here, in the third step, we look at a conflict situation as an object of analysis.

Analysis is breaking things down into their component parts to better understand the whole. It is a way of stepping back; disengaging from the situation to become more objective. It is linear, hierarchical, and detailed. If done jointly among the parties, analysis enables them to work together to address the conflict.

The analysis explores the conflict across these dimensions:

- Subject
- The parties
- Decision criteria
- Categories and types
- Attributes

The analysis begins with a definition of the subject and identification of the parties or stakeholders and their wants, interests, and needs. It continues with an identification of the criteria that will be used to decide on a resolution.

You continue to increase your knowledge by categorizing and qualifying the conflict by looking at its attributes. The goal is to define the kind of conflict you are facing so you can apply the right tools and techniques, in keeping with the principle of situational management.

Of course, we don't want to over analyze. There is a subjective decision as to how much time and effort you will spend analyzing. What does the situation call for? If the conflict is simple and the parties to it have worked together before it is likely that the analysis will be done in minutes, very informally. If the conflict is complex, important and intense, then it may take days or weeks to do the analysis. Make sure you document each conflict to some degree so that you can evaluate your conflict management process over time.

Use the categories, types, and attributes in this chapter and in the chapter on Conflicts in Projects to better understand your conflict.

Conflict Examples

Two conflict examples that we will refer to as we explore the types of conflicts we encounter in projects appear in the following. Reflect on your own projects conflicts as you read on. See how you can do something to make your process better.

The Wedding: Sit Down vs. Buffet

> **Context:** *A project to plan and put on a formal wedding celebration for 200–250 people with a limited budget*
>
> **Parties:** *The couple, their parents, advisors, and suppliers (wedding facilitators, caterers etc.).*
>
> **Content Issue:** *Sit down dinner preceded by hors d'oeuvre buffet vs. dinner buffet preceded by passed hors d'oeuvres.*
>
> **Positions:** *(1) It has to be a formal dinner; (2) It should be a "nice" hors d'oeuvres and cocktail hour followed by an open buffet.*
>
> **Decision criteria:** *Cost, comfort, image, food quality and quantity, mood, and expectations.*
>
> **Conflict source:** *Different perceptions of the way a wedding should be designed; taste.*
>
> **Resolution alternatives:** *(1) Sit down diner preceded by hors d'oeuvre buffet; (2) Buffet preceded by passed hors d'oeuvre; and (3) hybrid solution.*

The Financial Credit Project: Alternative Approaches

> **Context:** *A program to implement a commercial credit management system in a global financial organization with the need to get a handle on how much exposure the firm had to various families of clients and across industries, characteristics, regions, and countries.*

> **Content issue:** *Whether to replace a variety of differing credit management systems across business units around the world or to minimally change existing systems while accomplishing the objective of a global view of credit relationships for use in decision making.*

> **Parties:** *Two opposing groups of designers in the IT application development organizations, a product manager and the team, senior executive management, operations and administrative management, lending/account officers, among other stakeholders in the program.*

> **Positions:** *(1) We need to replace all of the systems in order to get a reliable centralized data base; and (2) Avoid replacement of existing systems.*

> **Decision criteria:** *Information reliability and accessibility, financial exposure control, control of technology, speed to implementation, technical feasibility, sustainability, cost, disruption of operations, security, effect on client relationships, performance improvement, etc.*

> **Resolution alternatives:** *(1) centralized system with common processes across all business units; and (2) a central repository fed by independent systems.*

The Subject and Causes

The analysis begins with the identification of the subject and issues. Conflict subjects may be design choices, vendor selection, differences regarding objectives and their priorities among many others. The conflict types enumerated in the "Conflicts in Projects" chapter represent the typical subjects.

To get to the real issue, "Each conflict situation should be closely examined so that underlying causes can be recognized in order to achieve resolution as swiftly and completely as possible. "The parties are requested to identify all the main issues or cues that caused the conflict" (Al-Tabtabai, Alex, & Abou-alfotouh, 2001).

The conflict type is analyzed to identify specific issues. For example in the case of a design conflict, the specific issues might be differences with regard to technology selection, cost, color, shape, size, ease of use, etc. With regard to a conflict over a performance review the issues may include adherence to schedule and budget constraints, customer satisfaction, the quality of peer relationships, etc.

With the issues identified, the parties can avoid speaking in generalities and be focused on relevant facts, alternatives, and priorities.

Beware. The subject that presents itself on the surface may be a smoke screen for other subjects; dig deep to determine the "real" subject. For example, while design presents itself as the subject, the real subject may be about the approach, tool, or vendor that might be implied by the selected design. Sometimes the real subject is about authority—who has the authority to dictate the design—as opposed to the design itself.

By drilling down into the details, it is likely that a cause that is not directly related to the presenting issue will be identified. For example, if in analyzing the issues in the design conflict it is found that none are substantive, it is likely that design is not the real subject. Then it becomes possible to get on with the work to identify and address the real issues.

The Parties and Their Interests, Needs, Positions, Wants

A subject is not enough on its own to create a conflict. There have to be people. The parties are the people involved in the conflict; the stakeholders. The principle parties are those who are directly involved, other parties include people who have varying degrees of interest and influence.

For each of the parties, make sure you know what their interests, roles, and authority are. Roles and authority were discussed in the chapter on "Conflicts in Projects." Here we will discuss interests and positions.

For there to be a conflict, there must be different positions held by the parties. A position is a point of view or mental attitude, neutral, for or against something. It is an opinion held in opposition to another. It represents a "want."

Positions are on perceived needs or interests. Interests are driven by the perceived impact the parties will take from the conflict and its resolution. Interests reflect what the parties really want as an outcome.

In the case of a conflict over design alternatives, the parties may start with the positions that they each want a different alternative. When we take the time to analyze the parties' positions and interests, we get results like those in the following table:

Position	Interest	Priorities and Fallback
I want the design that makes use of the latest technology.	To avoid costly upgrade or replacement when the technology becomes obsolete. To take advantage of efficiencies and cost savings.	Moderate priority. I would accept a design that is easily upgradable.
I want the design that offers the greatest ease of use.	To minimize training and support costs. To maximize productivity of the people using the product.	High priority. Open to some negotiation.
I want the design that has the lowest cost of development.	To fit within existing capital budget constraints.	High priority. Capital budget constraints are inflexible.
I want the design that has the lowest cost of ownership.	To maximize financial benefits. To make justification of the selection of the design easy.	Moderate priority. Open to trade-offs as long as there is a financial benefit.
I want a design that enables me to use existing tools and facilities.	To minimize costs and risk.	Moderate priority.

To highlight the importance of identifying the interests as opposed to just the positions "a story is commonly told about two children fighting over an orange. Both children take the position that they need (and deserve) the whole orange. If the mother listens to the two children's' positions, she will likely decide that one child deserves the orange more than the other—giving the whole orange to one—or maybe she will cut the orange in half, giving each a part.

> But the story goes on to explain that one child actually wanted the orange to eat, while the other wanted the rind for a science project. Had the children explained their underlying reasons for wanting the orange—that is, had they explained their **interests**—a win-win solution could have been found that would have given both children everything they wanted.

> "Although this is a simple story, people in conflict confuse positions and wants or interests all the time. They define what they want in all-or-nothing terms, take overly simple views of the problem, and seek solutions that meet their positions one hundred percent, without considering the views of the other side as important or legitimate. When people focus on one-dimensional positions—I want this or I don't want that—conflicts tend to appear to be unavoidably win-lose in nature, since the opponent almost always holds the opposite position. If the parties work to clarify WHY they want or do not want something, however, it often turns out that the parties' interests are, at least in part, compatible. This makes negotiating a solution—or at least a partial solution—much easier (Conflict Research Consortium, 1998)

Needs are the true motivators behind interests and positions. When you analyze your interests and the interests of the other parties, look for the underlying need. For example, in a design conflict, there is the need to be able to justify the selection based on financial criteria.

Put your own position in writing to make sure you really know what it is and why you hold it. It will help you to communicate it clearly. Think about and write what You may or may not want to share your full analysis with the other parties, but doing the work for yourself is valuable, as it will help you to better understand your po If the situation warrants it, you might help the other party to articulate his or her positions, interests, and priorities by asking questions to elicit them. They can be as simple as, "Would you mind telling me why you want that and how important it is to you in comparison to the other things you want?"

Criteria

The identification of wants, interests, and needs leads into an identification of the criteria to be used in the decision making. Conflict resolution implies decision making. Decisions must be made to resolve conflicts and disputes. Every position is held, and every decision is made based on criteria, which may or may not be consciously known.

What are the criteria? They are rules, standards, or tests that are the basis for decisions or judgments. They fall out of the identification of the parties' positions and interests. Analysis makes sure that the criteria are consciously known.

In a conflict over whether an estimate is accurate or not, the criteria might be the degree to which a set of estimate checklist items have been addressed, past experience of the estimators, the rationality of assumptions, the degree to which risk analysis has been done and used to refine the estimate.

Other criteria may be the degree to which the estimate meets a deadline or budget constraint or the degree to which the boss, sponsor, or client likes the estimate. These are criteria for whether to accept the estimate, but they do not address its accuracy. Make sure the right conflict is being addressed using the right decision criteria.

The Conflict Taxonomy

Once you have a solid sense of what the conflict is about, define it in terms of its category (is it content or relationship focused?) and attributes (e.g., complexity, intensity, importance, time pressure and intractability, certainty, reversibility, and degree of competitiveness) to better understand it. For each of these attributes identify where your conflict fits on a continuum from low to high.

Major Categories: Content and Relationship Centered

There are two major categories of conflicts: content and relationship centered. Before diving into the content determine whether your conflict is truly about the content or whether the content is a smoke screen that is hiding a relationship-based issue. As you work through the content, be aware of the tendency to devolve into relationship or emotional conflict.

Content Centered

In content-centered conflicts there is disagreement about an external object—an idea, requirements, criteria, design, way of doing something, a disturbing behavior, choice of a supplier, estimates, risk assessments, when to adjust the temperature, etc. The parties often have a common objective—resolve the content conflict and get on with the work.

Relationship Centered (Emotional) Conflict

Relationship- or emotion-centered conflict is conflict in which the content is secondary to the feelings experienced by the parties. There is animosity that is often based on anger, fear, and greed, or strong attachment to one's position or jealousy.

Every conflict has a relationship component but relationship centered conflicts are distorted by emotional reactions and personality clashes. Content conflicts may develop into relationship conflicts and, similarly, a series of disputes and intractable content conflicts may arise out of relationship conflicts.

In the wedding conflict example, the conflict can easily slip into the emotional realm when some parties refuse to listen to the other parties, or treat them with disdain or use tactics like "well I am paying for this event and I am going to call the shots." In conflict over alternative designs, if one party fears that he or she will lose autonomy or is strongly anchored in his or her position because of belief in a particular design philosophy, emotions may take over.

Knowing whether you are dealing with content centered conflict or conflict that is more or less influenced by politics, emotions, and personalities helps in three ways: (1) It gives you the opportunity to think about how you and others are likely to behave; (2) It makes for more realistic expectations; and (3) It gives you time to think about what to do to refocus a relationship conflict onto content or to step out of it completely if there is no content.

Emotional intelligence is needed to enable each individual to be responsive to his or her own emotions and the emotions of others and to avoid reactive behavior. We will explore Emotional Intelligence in more depth in a later chapter on the People Side of Conflict Management.

Conflict Attributes

Within the major categories and across the conflict types there are attributes to help you better understand the different kinds of conflicts that arise in projects:

- Complexity—makes conflicts difficult to manage
- Intensity—How heated is the conflict?
- Intractability—How resistant to resolution is the conflict?
- Importance—To what degree does the success of the project rely on an optimal resolution?
- Time pressure—How quickly is a resolution needed?
- Certainty/uncertainty—To what degree can you be sure of the outcome of applying the resolution?
- Reversibility—How easy is it to change the decision?
- Competitiveness—How likely are the parties to be competitive as opposed to collaborative?

The remainder of this chapter explores each of these attributes.

Complexity

Disputes and conflicts lie on a continuum stretching from minor disagreements that are easy to settle, to major, long-term deeply rooted disagreements requiring far more effort to resolve, if they are resolvable at all. This continuum is used as a means for deciding which conflict management approach is right for the situation—generally, the more complex the conflict the more formal the approach.

Note that, often, poorly managed minor disputes can lead to complex, long-term conflicts. Also, chronic minor disputes may be symptoms of larger, more complex conflicts.

While the content is a factor, the conflict's complexity is primarily influenced by factors such as the number of parties and their relationships to one another, including roles (project manager, functional manager, sponsor, client, performers and vendors), hierarchies (for example, superiors and subordinates; differences in authority to make binding decisions), and organization unit alignments. These factors are covered in the chapter on Conflicts in Projects.

To get a sense of complexity, imagine a conflict among key team members from sales, delivery, and customer service groups over how to approach a client. Once the conflict is resolved, the parties will work together for months or longer to satisfy the client. The situation is complex because of the relationships between the current decision and immediate, mid-range and long-term effects of the decision and the way the decision making was handled. If the person with the most authority or the best sales skills dictates an approach without convincing the others, there are predictable fallouts—lack of motivation, potential for readdressing the same conflict over and over again and more. The fact that the parties are from different groups and that the sales group's representative has the authority to make the decision adds to the complexity.

To most effectively resolve any conflict consider complexity before taking well intentioned action that may be disruptive.

See Appendix A for a method for determining conflict complexity.

Intensity

Intensity is concentration of power or force, having or displaying a feature to an extreme degree as in *the heat is intense.* In conflict management, it refers to the degree of effort and stress involved in addressing the conflict. Emotional reactivity and stress are often associated with intense conflicts.

In general, the intensity of conflict increases the more the impact of its resolution affects the project outcome, and particularly the wellbeing of the parties. For example, if one of the parties perceives that he or she will lose face, have their next performance review be negative, or be fired, that party will tend be more emotionally reactive and fight for his or her way. Conditions, such as the past relationships among the parties and the degree to which the parties are competing with peers or subordinates and superiors in a hierarchy, are what influence intensity.

Intensity is both influenced by and affects the choice of influencing style (whether to use expertise, authority, work challenge, friendship, promotion, or financial rewards to influence the outcome) and conflict resolution style (forcing, collaboration/confrontation, compromise, smoothing and avoidance). For example, the greater the intensity the greater a person with the power may rely on his or her authority to make the decision or employ a forcing style rather than a more collaborative one. The use of a forcing style by one party may cause others to react defensively.

Intractable Conflicts

Intractable conflicts are high intensity, high complexity conflicts.

"Intractable conflicts, broadly defined, are intense, deadlocked, and resistant to de-escalation or resolution. They tend to persist over time, with alternating periods of greater and lesser intensity. Intractable conflicts come to focus on needs or values that are of fundamental importance to the parties. The conflict pervades all aspects of the parties' lives, and they see no way to end it short of utterly destroying the other side. Each party's dominant motive is to harm the other. Such conflicts resist common resolution techniques, such as negotiation, mediation, or diplomacy. (Conflict Research Consortium, 2000).

Fortunately, this type of conflict is not very common in project management, organizational, or personal relationships. However, it does occur and when it does it challenges project managers to be able to get their projects done without getting involved in long term political issues that have little or nothing to do with their projects. For example, two groups (e.g., manufacturing and design engineering, sales and marketing, application development and business analysis) in the same organization with parallel or overlapping responsibilities can have an ongoing feud across many years because of different perspectives and performance philosophies or values. Two individuals may be rivals with different opinions, personality differences, and conflicting ambitions.

Case Example: Financial Credit Project Interorganizational Issues

Imagine the following scenario in the financial credit project. There was an intractable conflict regarding the roles of a central, corporate IT application development department and a project management/business analysis organization that was responsible for project administration and reporting as well as requirements analysis and definition. The head of the IT application development department wanted control over the project management and requirements functions while the head of the project management/ business analysis group, obviously, took an opposing position.

Things got so crazy that key IT people assigned to the project as development team leaders were instructed to not attend meetings chaired by the project manager assigned by the project management group. There was a major conflict over the form that requirements documentation should take. There were constant arguments regarding detailed issues in requirements documents that could have been resolved easily if left to the regular team members.

The intractable conflict could not be resolved without a senior executive decision and a reorganization to resolve it.

Managing the Current vs. Ultimate Dispute

When we recognize an intractable conflict, we must address it while dealing with its current manifestation in a specific short-term dispute. The current dispute is what needs to be resolved to move forward. The intractable conflict must be resolved or, at least, its effects remediated, in order to remove causes of future disputes and keep disputes from escalating, as the focus on content is lost to the intractable conflict's emotionality.

In the financial credit project case, the product/program manager stepped in and made it clear to the IT head that the situation he was creating was untenable and childish. The person from IT was confronted with the strong statement that unless he dealt with the organizational issue in the appropriate forums the product/program manager would escalate to the senior sponsor (a powerful executive vice president from the business whose career was on the line with the program's success) with recommendations that the IT development work be taken away from the corporate IT group and outsourced.

The IT head was not pleased, but he got the message and backed off. The various disputes were left to be handled by the team leads and performers and the project ran smoothly. Note that the product/program manager was not enticed into the broader intergroup conflict. His interest was in getting the work done in the most effective way in his scope of control. He was quite satisfied to eliminate the symptoms of the broader conflict.

Importance

Importance is a measure of how the success of the project relies on an optimal resolution. For example, the importance of a decision to choose a project strategy is high because the strategy will set the stage for the entire project and drive future decisions. A go/no-go decision made at any time is obviously very important. Any conflict resolution that drives other decisions is important.

Generally, as importance increases, there is a greater likelihood that people will become reactive. There is more at stake. The parties may feel threatened by the potential fallout of a bad decision or more strongly about the need to "do it their way."

Time pressure

Time pressure is a factor to be considered because as with importance, it tends to influence emotional reactivity. It also affects the amount of time available for analysis and coming to consensus. The greater the time pressure the more important it is to focus on the content issue at hand and avoid panic or unproductive forcefulness that may come from a false sense of urgency to resolve the issue.

You can manage the amount of time available by predicting and forcing conflicts early in project life.

Certainty and Uncertainty

Decisions bring conflicts to closure—whether by having a resolution or by deciding to live without one.

Decisions fall into two classes regarding the conditions surrounding them: (1) Decisions under certainty, where there is enough information to make a binding decision with a high degree of confidence in the outcome; and (2) Decisions under uncertainty: where there are many unknowns and no way to know what could occur in the future to effect the results of a decision.

An example of a decision under certainty is the decision to turn up the water temperature while taking a shower. There is a high level of certainty that it will make the water warmer after a brief delay. In a more project-oriented context, in the decision to delay the start of a six month construction project until the early spring there is a high degree of confidence that adverse weather conditions (snow and frozen ground) will not interfere with the project (assuming that the project is taking place outside of the hurricane zone).

Decisions in conflict situations are often decisions under uncertainty. We work in complex systems where it is impossible to fully know the outcome of an action. For example, when a decision regarding trade-offs on features and functions of a product is made there is uncertainty about the resulting impact of the decision on the overall level of satisfaction that the product's users will have. When a decision is made to accept an optimistic estimate to resolve a conflict between a functional manager and project manager the result on the ability of the project team to complete the project on schedule and budget is uncertain.

The greater the uncertainty of the decision the more difficult it is for the parties to come to agreement because each may have their own perceptions of the probabilities of different outcomes. Later as we discuss cultural norms, we will see how uncertainty may influence behavior.

Reversibility

A decision is easily reversible when it is possible to alter it without undo cost and disruption in the future. A decision is irreversible if it significantly reduces one's future choices. Some decisions are absolutely irreversible while most have varying degrees of reversibility.

Agreement regarding a reversible decision is easier to arrive at than one regarding an irreversible decision. The parties are more likely to be willing to move ahead knowing that if uncertain conditions evolve differently than expected they can revisit the decision without incurring significant cost. If on the other hand the decision is relatively irreversible, the parties will generally want more certainty or some greater incentive to move from their position to a compromise position to resolve the conflict. For example, a project manager is likely to take a chance and accept an alternative candidate being offered by a functional manager for a position if there is a strong likelihood that the candidate can be replaced with minimal cost if he or she doesn't work out.

Reversibility is influenced by two principle factors, stage in the project life cycle and expectations.

In projects, the stage in the project life cycle during which a decision is made affects the reversibility of the decision. For example, a decision made in an early stage of a project to include a particular feature in a product is highly reversible until the feature is designed into the product. It becomes relatively irreversible once it is built into the product.

With this in mind, it is a good practice in projects to avoid unnecessary conflict over what should be in or out of the product during the definition of requirements until there is solid information regarding cost, quality, and schedule information regarding the feature.

In our wedding case, decisions like the color of table linens may be reversible until just before the wedding. While other decisions, like the date, location and the nature of a custom wedding dress are increasingly irreversible as the event approaches.

In projects senior management and client expectations may make otherwise reversible decisions irreversible. For example, in a conflict over whether to provide even a "ball park" estimate or not, the perception that sponsor expectations will be irreversibly set by the high-level estimate can have a major influence.

The Degree of Competition: Contests

In analyzing your conflict, it is useful to have a sense of the degree to which the parties will be competitive as opposed to collaborative. This attribute influences intensity and intractability.

A contest is "a struggle for superiority or victory" (Contest, n.d.). Contests promote competition in which the skill of the players and luck are combined to decide the outcome.

When a conflict is in reality a contest between competing parties, in which one will win and the other lose, as opposed to a disagreement regarding ideas, there is divisiveness.

Contests are hard to avoid when the parties tend to have strong egos and the desire to win. While these personal attributes can be very healthy, they can bring with them a need to turn every dispute into a contest. It is better to burn off the competitive energy with extracurricular activities—chess, pool, computer based games, etc.—than to let them play out, often unconsciously, in the "real world" of work or relationship.

Knowing that the conflict with a possible win-win outcome is turning into a contest helps to avoid unnecessary competition. As a conflict manager or facilitator, you can make the parties aware of their attitudes and focus them on their common interests. You can highlight the negative effects of unnecessary competition, for example, the tendency to adhere to positions even though they may not be optimal or where there are not significant differences between positions.

Zero-sum and Non–zero-sum Conflicts

As a means for minimizing the occurrence of unnecessary contests, it is useful to classify your conflict as zero-sum or non–zero-sum.

Not all conflicts are subject to win-win solutions. Whether the conflict is zero-sum or non–zero-sum influences the relationships between the parties and their strategies.

Zero-sum

A zero-sum conflict has a winner and one or more losers. There is a fixed winnable resource. Therefore whatever one party wins is lost by another. The sum of what is gained and what is lost is zero. Chess is a good example of a zero-sum game. Someone wins, someone loses, or there is a draw. A conflict that rests on a decision for something being done in one of two ways or a choice between two candidates or designs is a zero sum conflict.

Knowing you are managing a zero-sum conflict gives helps you choose an approach that, if you are on one side or another, improves your chance of winning. For example, you are unlikely to seek to share your design with a competing design team to come up with an optimal solution. If you are managing above these teams, you might choose to change the game to incentivize collaboration for the overall benefit of the organization as a higher value than winning. You might have the teams periodically share their ideas and interim results to promote cross-fertilization, and through that, better results. In the end, one team's design would be selected.

In the movie *Extraordinary Measures*, teams competing to develop a pharmaceutical cure for a disease, cut costs and reduce time lines by opening unfinished research to mutual scrutiny to select the approach that was farthest along. They agreed (or were ordered to agree) to forego their own approach to collectively pursue the one that was most likely to be successful in the shortest time for the least cost.

Non–zero-sum Games

"Monopoly (if it is <u>not</u> played with the intention of having just one winner), is a non–zero-sum game: all participants can win property from the "bank." In principle, in Monopoly, two players could reach an agreement and help each other in gathering a maximum amount from the bank. That is not really the intention of the game, but I hope I have made the distinction clear: in non–zero-sum games the total amount gained is variable, and so both players may win (or lose). When they can both win by cooperating in some way, we might say that their cooperation creates a *synergy*" (Conflict Research Consortium, 2000).

Non–zero-sum games promote collaboration to maximize the measurable rewards each party receives (money, recognition, time off, etc.)

Effective conflict management implies promoting collaboration, where it is possible and where it is not (as in zero-sum gains) promoting fair competition based on respect and values like honesty and fairness so as to enable competitors to work together in the future.

Chapter Summary

This chapter has explored a conflict as a multifaceted object. To situationally manage, you must know your situation, analysis provides the knowledge.

We identified and described the things you need to know about your conflict to properly address it. You need to know your subject/type, the parties, and their interests, and decision-making criteria as well as whether your conflict is content or relationship centered. You need to qualify your conflict with regard to its attributes to know the nature of your conflict.

These are the attributes:

- complexity,
- intensity,
- intractability,
- importance,
- time pressure,
- certainty,
- reversibility, and
- degree of competition.

These apply across the conflict types—schedule, priorities, resources, technical, administrative, personality, cost, performance, and supplier selection.

The analysis enables a stepping back from reactive behavior to gain greater knowledge upon which to base decisions

Chapter 6

Seek to Understand: Conflict Styles and Approaches

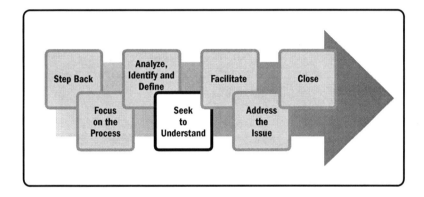

"Seek to understand, then to be understood" (Covey, 2004).

Everyone is alike and is, at the same time, as different from everyone else as snowflakes are from one another.

Chapter Overview

This chapter and the next represent the fourth step in the conflict management process—Seeking to Understand. Seeking to understand extends analysis from the conflict as an object to the nature of the participants.

Have you ever wondered why a person did something you found to be completely irrational and very negative? "What were they thinking? Were they even thinking at all?"

The conflict styles or approaches discussed in this chapter and the issues covered in the chapter the "People Side of Conflict Management" provide answers.

There is significant diversity in culture, thinking styles, conflict style, degree of emotional intelligence, knowledge, and more. People have different personalities and behavioral tendencies even in an environment where everyone is from the same culture and shares common beliefs and values.

To better manage conflict, seek to understand how these differences will affect the reasons for disagreements, and the way you and others respond to one another and how you generally behave when confronted.

This chapter is based on the Thomas-Kilman Conflict Mode model. We will define the model and its styles, discuss the ideal approaches in different situations, explore how the choice of approach influences outcomes and relationships, and discuss motivations to use one approach or another.

Conflict Style and Approach

Conflict style is the distinctive way you behave in conflict situations. It is a general tendency; the collection of behaviors you typically exhibit when in conflict. Approach, on the other hand, is the method used to accomplish something. Your style influences your approach, but it is not the only influence. You do best to consciously flex your style to choose an approach that is suited to your situation. For example, within a project, some situations may call for one of the parties to avoid conflict while another is pushing for a position he or she values.

Behavioral Models

"Models are always wrong. But they can be useful" (Box & Draper, 1987, p. 424).

Behavioral models are powerful means to gain understanding. But be careful. They are very useful in identifying typical tendencies and in turning people towards self-analysis and awareness. They become harmful when they are used to stereotype people and over simplify the complex nature of individuals and the way they behave in relationships. Let's explore how people typically operate in conflict.

The Conflict Mode Model

There are a number of styles inventories and conflict approach models. The Thomas-Kilman Conflict Mode Instrument (TKI) is a relatively simple and accurate style inventory that has become a virtual standard for defining the prevailing styles that people have in addressing conflict.

To determine an individual's style, the model uses a basic instrument of 30 forced-answer questions (for example, "2. A. I try to find a compromise situation. Or B. I attempt to deal with all of his and my concerns." (Thomas & Kilman, n.d.). There are variations that add a scale of strength of traits. Results are interpreted to obtain a sense of an individual's tendency and comfort level regarding five conflict-handling modes.

The modes are defined using two dimensions (Figure 6-1): "(1) assertiveness: the extent to which the individual attempts to satisfy his own concerns; and (2) cooperativeness: the extent to which the individual attempts to satisfy the other person's

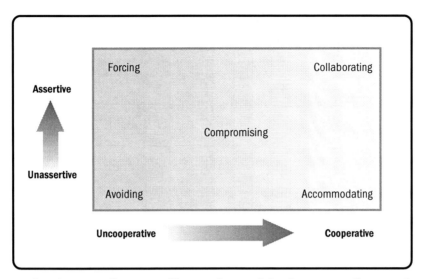

Figure 6-1: The Thomas-Kilman Conflict Modes Model (Thomas & Kilman, n.d.).

concerns" (Thomas & Kilman, n.d.). Each axis is a continuum with infinite degrees of assertiveness and infinite degrees of cooperativeness.

Further, people's assertiveness and cooperativeness change as the conflict becomes more intense and individuals become more or less stressed, anxious, or emotionally attached to their position, or fearful because of hierarchical- and power-based relationships. Therefore, the conflict handling modes are likely to be applied with varying degrees of intensity and may shift from situation to situation.

The five conflict handling modes are these:

Competing (Forcing)—An individual pursues his own concerns at the other person's expense. Power is used to win or defend a position believed to be right.

Accommodating—The opposite of competing. It is characterized by neglecting one's own concerns to satisfy the concerns of another. Motivations may be self-sacrifice; obeying another's orders, or yielding to another's point of view. Accommodating may also arise out of a value for cultivating long-term relationships and promoting buy-in for an ultimate solution.

Avoiding—The individual does not address the conflict. "Avoiding might take the form of diplomatically sidestepping an issue, postponing an issue until a better time or simply withdrawing from a threatening situation" (Thomas & Kilman, n.d., pp. 8–9).

Collaborating—The parties work together to identify and address their concerns. They find alternatives and solutions that might combine elements of all positions. They problem solve and negotiate.

Compromising—Here parties find a mutually acceptable solution. The parties are partially satisfied as they balance competing and accommodating. Parties give up some of their demands to accommodate one another; splitting the differences, they seek a quick middle ground solution.

"Some authors have suggested that there is a subtle difference between collaborating and another mode, confronting/problem solving" (Verma, 1996, p. 118). For our purposes, we will assume that collaborating implies that the parties are confronting the issue with problem solving and negotiating.

The Ideal Approach

While a collaborative approach might seem to be ideal, it is not the right approach for every situation.

To achieve win-win solutions and strong ongoing relationships, collaborating is often the way to go. However, consider what would happen if one person was a collaborator and everyone else were competitive. The collaborator would have to "convert" the others and get them to agree to a collaborative mode. This might be and usually is impractical, at least in addressing a relatively minor, short-term dispute or in the case of vendors competing for a job. Further, collaboration takes more time and effort than, say, forcing. Is the time available?

"All five modes are useful in some situations: each represents a set of useful social skills. Our conventional wisdom recognizes, for example, that often "two heads are better than one" (Collaborating). But it also says, "Kill your enemies with kindness" (Accommodating), "Split the difference" (Compromising) "Leave well enough alone" (Avoiding), "Might makes right" (Competing/Forcing). The effectiveness of a given conflict-handling mode depends upon the requirements of the specific conflict situation and the skill with which the mode is used" (Thomas & Kilman, n.d., p. 9).

Consider your own comfort level with the modes and the requirements of the situation and then act accordingly.

When to Use Which Mode

The following table contains guidelines for when to use and not use the five modes.

Mode	Use it	Do not use it
Competing/Forcing (authority- and power- based— Usually has a win-lose result; leaves a dominated party)	When speedy decision and action is required When unpopular actions may result When you know you are right and the issue is critical When you are dealing with people who won't cooperate When you have the power	When buy-in from all parties is needed to implement the resolution When long-term goals include promoting a collaboration that empowers stakeholders When you don't have power

Mode	Use it	Do not use it
Collaborative (usually results in a win-win result; takes more time, skill, patience and effort than other modes)	When it is important to find an optimal solution that result from merging aspects of multiple options and satisfies all parties When learning by understanding the other parties' positions and assumptions and testing your own is important When long term commitment to the resulting decision is important When cultivating long-term harmonious relationships among the parties is important	When time to a resolution is an essential factor When the parties are not committed to open discussion and cooperation When the parties are not skilled in a collaborative approach
Compromising (can lead to a lose-lose resolution where the parties agree to a watered down solution that ultimately satisfies no one, but may be quick and the result can be good enough)	When the resolution outcome is not of significant importance to warrant the time and effort involved in other, more assertive, approaches When the parties are strongly committed to their own mutually exclusive objectives (for example, labor negotiations or disputes over assignment of staff in a project) When trying to achieve a temporary solution to a complex issue When either competition or collaboration doesn't seem to be working	When the issue is critical and requires an optimal solution When the original positions are inflated and unrealistic When the commitment to implement the solution is doubted
Avoiding (may lead to a win-lose or lose-lose outcome, particularly if there is denial of the issue at hand, but may be quick and avoid unnecessary conflict)	When the issue is not worth the time and effort to engage in any of the other modes When the effort and potential damage to relationships are greater than the benefits When you realize that the other alternatives are as good as yours to address the issue at hand When the issue is a smoke screen or "red herring" for another issue	When the issue is important When the issue will not just go away or be resolved effectively without confronting it When not confronting the issue will lead to feelings of resentment, suppressed anger or an inability to truly support the way forward When avoiding will result in an image as being an easy mark
Accommodating (may lead to a win-lose or lose-lose outcome, particularly if there is a habitual tendency to accommodate others at one's own expense)	When it is clear that your position is incorrect or unreasonable When you want to satisfy the needs of others and maintain a cooperative relationship, for example you want a subordinate to gain experience and confidence or to learn from their own mistakes	When the issue is important When you are sure that the other parties' positions are inappropriate or would lead to sub-optimal resolutions When losing would lead to feelings of resentment, suppressed anger or an inability to support the way forward

How Conflict Mode Effects Outcome—A Trip to Abilene

The story of the Trip to Abilene provides a wonderful example of how people's conflict mode effect the outcome. It is an example of how failure to risk a conflict (accommodating and avoiding) can hurt.

Jerry Harvey tells of his experience while visiting his in-laws in Coleman, Texas. He, his wife, and her parents were sitting on the porch on a hot, 104°F (40°C), dusty afternoon, sipping cold lemonade and playing Dominoes, when his father-in-law suggested that they all get in the un–air-conditioned car and drive 53 miles to Abilene to eat dinner at the cafeteria. Jerry's wife said she thought it was a good idea and asked him what he thought. He was appalled at the idea, but did not say so. Instead, he and his mother-in-law agreed.

So, off they go to Abilene. The cafeteria was anything but a four-star restaurant. After a mediocre meal, a little heartburn, and a hot dusty drive, they returned to Coleman, exhausted. After a short while of silent cooling off, Harvey reports that he said, "Well, it was a great trip, wasn't it?" His mother-in-law disagreed. She thought it was horrible and that she just went along because the others wanted to go. She had wanted to stay home.

They soon discovered that none of them really wanted to go.

The father-in-law made the suggestion because he thought the others were bored, the others went along out of courtesy and not wanting to keep the group from doing what it wanted to do. Everyone wanted to please everyone else. No one wanted to risk a conflict (Harvey, 1988, pp. 17–43).

How many trips to Abilene do you go on? Are they fun?

The Abilene Paradox

The Abilene paradox is the phenomena of groups and organizations making decisions and taking action in contradiction to the data at hand. They go on to compound problems and go off in the wrong direction. The data (in particular, the parties' needs, wants, interests, facts, and opinions) are available, to the individuals, who keep it private rather than sharing it so the group can come to an effective agreement. In the TKI model, avoiding is identified as being low in assertiveness and cooperativeness.

What motivates a person to withhold the data that would make it possible for the group to come to an effective agreement, rather than one that sends them on a trip to Abilene? It might be lack of consciousness about the impact of <u>not</u> sharing, or fear of being responsible for actions that may be caused by his or her input, or fear of being different and separated from the group. It could be because of low self-csteem ("My input won't matter"), anger expressed passive-aggressively, or laziness ("It's not worth the effort to say what I'm thinking"). As in the story, the motivation might be "niceness," wanting to be polite and accommodating.

The paradox, Harvey points out, is that the fear of being held responsible for making a poor decision creates a certainty of making a poor decision. The desire to be "nice" leads to sub-optimal results when there is no communication and collaboration.

Why? By avoiding conflict you disenable the exchange that would enable a good decision. The failure to speak up helps to perpetuate poor decisions, blaming and unnecessary conflict.

In this analysis, the focus was on avoiding conflict and how that can be damaging. It may be just as damaging to insist on your way by bowling over the opposition or to spend more time than it is worth collaborating or trying to save time by compromising when the compromise leads to a sub-optimal solution that is worse than either of the conflicting alternatives.

So, in conflicts, speak up, offer your information, and seek optimal resolutions using the right mode(s) for the situation.

Organization Cultures and Conflict Styles

Individuals are not the only ones with styles. Organizations often have styles of their own that effect conflict management. Here we will describe passive-aggressive and authoritarian cultures. Be aware of their influences.

Passive-Aggressive

A very common form of avoidant conflict style is found as a trait in organization culture. It is passive-aggressive behavior that takes the form of people saying they publically agree to something and then privately disparaging it after the decision has been made. In passive-aggressive cultures, at the meeting to select the design approach, when asked if everyone is "on board" everyone expresses their agreement. As soon as the meeting is over, in small groups, people are saying things like "That will never work."

If this style is operating in your organization, bring it to light and cultivate the cooperative atmosphere required for collaboration and honesty.

Authoritarian Cultures

In authoritarian and competitive cultures where power is exercised freely and there is top down decision making and control, there is a tendency to find people with competitive or forcing styles to have their way, if they are in the right place in the hierarchy. If they are not high enough in the power structure and they play out their natural style, they may encounter strong opposition from peers and penalties from superiors. Have you seen two people exercising forcing behavior where one is the ultimate decision maker? It is not a healthy situation for the one on the bottom nor is it healthy for the organization. The decision is pretty much of a foregone conclusion and the person at the lower end of the hierarchy is likely to withdraw and therefore not provide useful information or alternatives.

It is common to find many people with avoiding or accommodating styles, or people who take on these approaches in-order to survive, at lower levels in the hierarchy in an authoritarian culture.

Winning and Losing—Motivation to Use a Conflict Mode

In both passive-aggressive and authoritarian cultures, there is often a distorted view regarding winning and losing and the motivation those views bring to the parties. What is your motivation to choose a particular conflict mode in a given situation? In conflicts, the motivation is often to win. But, sometimes wining is losing! It all depends of what you mean by winning and who you include in the winner's circle.

Therefore, choosing the right mode requires being clear about what "winning" and "losing" mean.

A win is when the outcome of a dispute satisfies the needs of the parties <u>and</u> their organization. If one consciously avoids a conflict and the result is a workable outcome, both parties win, even though one party's <u>position </u>has "lost." In a project as in all personal relationships, everyone wins when the outcome satisfies higher-level values, goals, and objectives and meets individual needs.

Don't win the battle at the expense of the war. If you win the dispute but lose the respect and trust of someone in an ongoing relationship, there is loss. Which is more important; the short-term win or the long-term loss? The answer depends on the situation and the answer will dictate your choice of approach.

If someone bullies his or her way through based on authority, gamesmanship, or wins because others avoid and accommodate and the team fails to adopt the best design based on an objective assessment of alternatives, benefits, costs, and risks, the project and the organization losses. Depending on his or her values and the future impact of the decision on that person's career, the proponent may also lose.

Case Study: The Centralization Project

After attending a conference and having a couple of meetings with representatives of a consulting firm Amir "fell in love" with a design concept that required high consistency among branches, the acquisition of a major computer system to replace several existing systems and changes to business procedures and policies. The concept was elegant and the vendor promised installation and conversion of data from existing systems within a year.

Since Amir was the chief operating officer, he had the power to make the decision to pursue the change initiative and to prioritize it, fund it, and resource it, and motivate its execution. Amir's natural style in conflict was competitive; he was highly assertive, confident of his judgment and liked getting his way. He was not particularly sensitive to the relationship and cooperative side of the process.

He presented his ideas to the head of IT and to his other direct reports. When questions and objections arose, and the desire to study alternatives and assess risks, costs, and benefits, Amir made it clear that the team did not need negativity and defeatists. "We need to pull together and make this happen." "Let's get on with this and get it done." Knowing Amir and given his position of authority, no one said anything.

In the end, the project was chartered and the organization spent several millions of dollars and many person hours of effort. After three years, the project was scrapped with only half the branches converted and productivity in those branches far below expectations.

Note that it is not only the forcing style of the person in authority that causes disasters. Sometimes there is the belief that taking the time to plan, assess risk, and consider alternatives is a waste. Sometimes the cause is avoidant styles on the part of the people who have held back. Often it is a combination of all of them.

What might have happened if one or more of Amir's direct reports found a way to slow Amir down, make him confront some of the risks, and open his mind to alternative possibilities? Maybe they could have asked a key question or quickly provided an eye-opening possible negative scenario. If they had, the organization could have experienced a successful transformation and a successful project.

What are your examples of how habitual application of natural styles affected your projects and relationships? How might have flexing your style affected the outcome?

Analyzing Your Mode Choices

One of the powers of a conflict mode model is that it stimulates thinking about how style influences success. It opens the door to consciously choosing a situationally appropriate mode. Following is some good advice culled from the work of Thomas and Kilmann (TKI).

If your tendency is to be competitive and push for your way,

- Have you created a situation in which people are afraid of disagreeing with you or decide to avoid conflicts because they have given up on trying to influence you?
- Are people afraid to admit uncertainty and ignorance with you, presenting strong arguments with seemingly great confidence, even when it is inappropriate?
- If so, your strong leaning towards a competitive mode maybe having a detrimental effect and keeping you and your team from candidly exploring issues. Getting your own way may feel good for the moment but it is not always an effective way to manage conflict.

If you tend to be weak in confronting you may want to assess the reasons for it and get stronger in this area. You may want to reassess your power so you can appropriately exert your influence.

If you spend too much time discussing issues that are not worthy of the time and effort, you may be overdoing collaboration. Collaboration to reach consensus takes time and effort. Make sure it is worth it.

If you find that efforts at collaboration (for example, asking questions rather than making assertions and seeking discussion of process before engaging in the content) fail to engage the other parties you may be facing mistrust, competitiveness, ignorance or impatience and strong feelings. Look for subtle cues. Determine if it is time to shift your mode.

If you tend away from collaborative approach, you may be missing opportunities because you do not use conflicts and disputes as opportunities to transform relationships and achieve optimal solutions.

If you overdo compromise it may be a sign that you have lost track of long-term goals, quality principles and values and have succumbed to a desire to get a resolution even if it is ineffective. You may also fall into a competitiveness that focuses on trading and bargaining rather than a search for optimal solutions.

If, on the other hand, you tend to be weak in compromise mode, it may be because you are embarrassed to put forth your ideas, wants, and needs or because you find it hard to make concessions. People who have strong competitive tendencies find compromise difficult. Perfectionists find compromise difficult.

If you overdo avoiding, you are depriving your team of your inputs on issues. Confront the causes of your avoidance.

If on the other hand, you don't avoid conflicts with trivial issues or in which the benefits of confrontation are outweighed by the liabilities, then you risk bogging yourself and others down on an unnecessary number of issues.

If you overdo accommodating, you may harbor anger and resentment because you feel that your own ideas and concerns are not getting the attention they deserve. Like avoiding, excessive accommodating deprives the group of valuable input. It may be a sign that you are more eager to make people feel good than reaching an effective outcome. Seek balance between concern for people and concern for task.

If you fail to accommodate when appropriate, you may appear unreasonable and uncaring or incapable of backing off your position even when it is wrong. Caring for and about others is a trait that can be cultivated by setting it as a valued intention.

Chapter Summary

Know your tendency to force, avoid, accommodate, compromise, and collaborate in conflicts and make the point to choose an approach that, even if it is not your natural style, is best for the situation. Don't just act out of your habits and conditioning when that robs your team of the ideas and questions that may be the difference between optimal performance and failure.

Openly assessing conflict styles is a powerful part of team building and relationship management. At the start of a project, knowing that conflicts will likely arise, include a conflict styles assessment and a discussion about the implications of the styles and the modes of addressing conflicts. The model promotes an analysis of the process. It brings the parties together in the recognition of the dynamics that are at work as they seek to address their conflicts.

The choice of your process and the analysis of the type of conflict, its nature, and the specifics regarding the subject and environment, and the people involved put you in a strong position to select the approach that has the right balance between assertiveness and cooperation.

The next chapter goes deeper into the nature of the people involved in the conflict.

Chapter 7

The People Side of Conflict Management

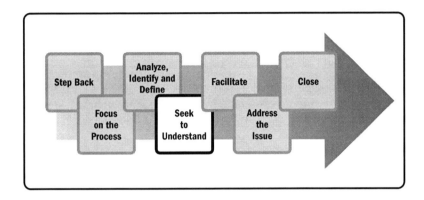

Chapter Overview

The keys to successful outcomes and healthy relationships are self-management and awareness of others.

In this and in the previous chapter, we seek to understand how you and the other parties are likely to behave and why. In the previous chapter, we explored one dimension of self-knowledge—conflict style.

This chapter explores **emotional intelligence** and the effect of frames or mental models and how they affect behavior. It looks at how **cognitive analysis** helps to minimize unnecessary conflict and enables effective resolutions. **Cultural differences** (diversity) and the way they influence your and other people's conflict behavior are also discussed.

Managing yourself in conflict is as critical a part of conflict management as managing others. In fact, without self-management, you will not be able to manage others. Cultivating your emotional intelligence (your awareness of your own and other people's emotions and the way they affect behavior) helps you avoid being emotionally reactive.

In applying cognitive analysis, emotional intelligence and the awareness of cultural influences, you are using the mindfulness and objectivity associated with stepping back. Collect your thoughts and act calmly and coolly to get the results you want.

Emotional Intelligence

Emotional intelligence (EI) reflects the ability to be aware of your own and other people's emotions and to avoid being emotionally reactive. It is the capacity to use the intellect to reason about emotions and by doing so to avoid emotion driven behavior. Emotion driven behavior can be damaging in conflict situations as it does not consider the impact of the behavior and is contrary to situational management and the desire for win-win results. Mindfulness is the foundation for EI.

EI is concerned with the way people recognize and regulate feelings (self-management) and the responses of others (social competence). Self-awareness enables self-management. Self-management and social awareness enable healthy relationships which enable effective conflict management.

Table 7–1 identifies the principle components of EI. Note that recognition or awareness enables, but does not guarantee regulation.

Self-recognition measures the degree to which people recognize their emotions and the reactive tendencies caused by them, has an accurate sense of their own capabilities, tendencies, and mental models and is relatively sure of themselves and their perceptions.

Self-regulation measure the ability to control behavior, adapt to changing circumstances, take initiative, work toward objectives and be trustworthy (truthful, keeping one's word, etc.).

Social competence reflects the degree to which the individual is socially aware and how well she manages relationships.

Social-awareness is measured by the degree to which one is empathetic (can pick up cues of how others are feeling and has a sense of the other as a person deserving of positive feelings and how those feeling may be influenced by one's

Table 7.1: Emotional Intelligence (Nair & Balasubramania, 2008)

	Self: Personal Competence	Other: Social Competence
Recognition	Self-Awareness Emotional self-awareness Accurate self-assessment Self-confidence	Social Awareness Empathy Service orientation Organisational awareness
Regulation	Self-Management Self-control Trustworthiness Conscientiousness Adaptability Achievement drive Initiative	Relationship Management Developing others Influencing Communication Conflict management Leadership Change catalyst Teamwork and collaboration

behavior), oriented toward service (has an objective the best possible outcome for others and the organization or environment as a whole), aware of the organization or environment (cognizant of how individual behavior is both influenced by and influences the organization or group).

How EI Effects Conflict Behavior

People with lower levels of EI will tend to react emotionally when they don't get their way. They will yell and pound the table or retreat into a fear-induced shell; they will do and say things that negatively affect others and tend to ignore the greater good in a blind charge to support their position and win at the expense of the organization, project, or group.

For example, in a dispute over whether to estimate a task at one or two calendar weeks, the estimator's manager insists that the estimate be one week. The estimator will be responsible for performing the task.

The employee "loses it," raises his voice, and begins a rant on how he is always squeezed and put into a position where he is constantly blamed for being late and forced to cut corners and deliver substandard results. If the manager has a low level of EI, that person is more likely to respond with something like, "Stop whining and wasting time that you could be spending on getting the job done" or "If you can't do it we'll find someone else who can" creating a spiraling anger cycle or cutting off any dialogue that might lead to a win-win resolution.

If the manager is more emotionally intelligent, then that person might respond with "I understand how angry this makes you, let's calm down, and discuss the issue. How about if we look at the assumptions and risks in both estimate options and see how we can come to an agreement that will satisfy the project need to meet the deadline and the needs of you and your team."

Alternatively, a manager with a high degree of EI might raise the issue differently. Instead of starting with insisting that the estimate be a week, she might have started the conversation by asking questions about the estimator's assumptions. She might have engaged the estimator in a challenge to see how the task can be done in a week.

If the employee had a high level of EI, he or she might have seen his or her rising anger and been able to avoid being driven by it.

In either case, the emotionally intelligent person will seek to avoid and defuse emotional responses by focusing on effective behavior, relationship skills, and project management skills to get to a resolution that satisfies the needs of the situation.

Improving Your EI

The key to EI is to cultivate greater mindfulness and the ability to step back, as described in the Foundation Concepts chapter. Mindfulness enables you to observe the arising of your emotions before they take over and drive behavior and to clearly observe the other party's demeanor. Then you can choose your behavior.

To improve your EI, practice mindfulness meditation and assess your tendency to be reactive and uncaring about the feelings of others.

Cognitive Analysis: Frames and Mental Models

With the ability to step back and avoid emotional reactivity comes the ability to apply knowledge and techniques to better understand where everyone is "coming from"; what is driving their behavior. There can be an open-minded exploration of multiple perspectives. This exploration dispels false impressions and helps to avoid misunderstandings that may create unnecessary conflicts. The result is a strong focus on communication and a higher degree of trust among the parties.

Cognitive analysis is a method for exploring frames and models to enable greater insight into why the parties take the positions they take. That insight in turn leads to greater ability to come to win-win outcomes that satisfy individual and collective needs. Before exploring cognitive analysis, we will define and discuss frames or mental models as these are the foundations of the cognitive approach.

When we looked at conflict styles, we saw that there are different ways of approaching conflict and that the choice of approach is influenced by each person's style. Behind the style are "frames" or mental models.

Now let's define some terms:

- "A frame is a set of assumptions or standards that motivate and give meaning to behavior. Frames are cognitive shortcuts that people use to help make sense of complex information. Frames help us to interpret the world around us and represent that world to others. They help us organize complex phenomena into coherent, understandable categories. When we label a phenomenon, we give meaning to some aspects of what is observed, while discounting other aspects because they appear irrelevant or counter-intuitive. Thus, frames provide meaning through selective simplification, by filtering people's perceptions and providing them with a field of vision for a problem" (Kaufmann, Elliott, & Shmueli, 2003).
- Mental models are "deeply ingrained assumptions, generalizations, or even pictures and images that influence how we understand the world and how we take action" (Senge, Kleiner, Roberts, Ross, & Smith, 1994, p. 8). They are beliefs, concepts, and assumptions.
- Open-mindedness is defined in terms of the degree to which people question their beliefs, explore the causes of their behavior, and are open to changing their mind.

- Reframing is purposefully managing frames to identify and address differences. For example, (1) helping the parties to identify themselves with a common organization or mission rather than with ones that set them apart from one another; or (2) making sure everyone agrees regarding the process they will use.

"The discipline of mental models starts with turning the mirror inward; learning to unearth our internal pictures of the world, to bring them to the surface and hold them rigorously to scrutiny. It also includes the ability to carry on 'learningful' conversations that balance inquiry and advocacy, where people expose their own thinking effectively and make that thinking open to the influence of others" (Senge et al., 1994, p. 9). *"Learningful" conversations* are dialogues that seek understanding rather than conclusions; this technique will be covered later.

Frames and mental models are the underlying thought systems that, often unconsciously, influence our behavior. For the purpose of simplicity, we will use the terms interchangeably.

Mental Models and Conflict

Framing a conflict is done to better understand events and to gain strategic advantage. It can be used to rationalize one's own position or to get others to understand and support an argument.

In the context of a conflict, we create frames to help us understand the following:

- why the conflict exists,
- what actions are important to the conflict,
- why the parties act as they do, and
- how we should act in response.

"During the evolution of a conflict, frames act as sieves through which information is gathered and analyzed, positions are determined (including priorities, means, and solutions), and action plans developed. Depending on the context, framing may be used to conceptualize and interpret, or to manipulate and convince" (Kaufmann et al., 2003).

Experts recommend paying particular attention to these six frames:

Identities—What do the parties think about themselves? How do their perceived group affiliations affect their decision making process and their filtering of information?

The way they/we characterize others—Includes stereotypes that attribute either positive or negative characteristics to others which may or may not be in agreement with their own self-identity.

The concepts of power—Determine the way parties view which forms of power are legitimate and how much power they have in effecting change and making decisions.

The process—The way conflict should be handled. What options are available and which are most likely to get the desired results.

Risk—The way the parties perceive the degree of uncertainty and the impact of potential events.

Loss vs. gain beliefs—It is common that parties to serious disputes "focus on the threat of potential loss rather than on opportunities for gains. People tend to react differently to a proposed action when its expected consequences are framed in terms of losses as opposed to gains, where preventing a perceived loss is often more salient and more highly valued than capturing a commensurate gain" (Kaufmann et al., 2003).

Applying Framing

Let's see how this might work in the context of a conflict over a project schedule. The direct parties are a project manager and the manager. The project is to get a new product line into the market in order to generate profits as quickly as possible. It could just as easily be getting an oil well pumping or to put on an event.

The project manager has spent a week or so working with team members to develop a well thought out estimate which considered quality, time and cost trade-offs, risk and the availability of resources and facilities.

The project manager's manager has met with the project sponsor and has come away with the impression that project completion must be within a very aggressive timeframe and a tight budget constraint. The sponsor and client view resource constraints and risk as the manager's problem. Further, they assume that quality will be high, though have not adequately defined just what that means.

The project manager perceives the manager to be a coward who, out of self-interest, consistently fails to adequately push back when confronted with unrealistic demands from above. In the past, this has led to project failures, dissatisfied clients and sponsors, and severely over worked and disheartened performers.

The manager perceives himself to be a realist and the project manager to be an immature optimist who spends more time figuring out how to avoid making hard to fulfill commitments than in fulfilling them. He sees the project manager and his team as having no real appreciation for the real-world practicalities that must be dealt with.

The project manager sees himself as being relatively powerless in influencing his boss and getting his boss to influence those who really are in charge. The manager perceives himself as being powerless in convincing the sponsor and client that what they are asking for is unrealistic.

The project manager thinks he has one shot at presenting the estimate and plan and has no alternative other than to succumb to the demands from above or quit. The boss thinks there can be a negotiation between himself and the project manager that would find a way of meeting expectations, but that in the end he will make the decision.

The project manager sees the most serious risks as the delivery of a product that fails in the field and the unnecessary disruption of work on other projects. The manager sees the most severe risk as the loss of the sponsor, who might go elsewhere to get his demands met.

Without taking a step back to assess these attitudes, it is highly likely that the conflict will result in a repetition of the past—late delivery, poor quality, burned out workers, reinforced negative perceptions.

So what can happen?

Either party or an outside facilitator (perhaps someone from a project management office) can raise the issue of experience and how there is a pattern of behavior that if not addressed will result in an unsatisfactory experience. If they can convince the parties to take a new tack and explore their mental models they may be able to find a way to work together to provide an argument for the manager to take to the sponsor to get him to change his expectations. This would require that the manager take the project manager more seriously and change his perception regarding the sponsor's flexibility and values. It would require the project manager to open to a change in perception of his boss and of the conflict management process itself.

Cognitive analysis and the evaporating cloud method discussed later in this chapter can be used to support the exploration of frames.

Cognitive Analysis

In the chapter Analysis: The Nature of a Conflict, we introduced the concept of positions, wants, interests, and needs, here we discuss how they relate to cognitive analysis and how we can use the evaporating cloud method to uncover them and resolve conflicts more easily. A full treatment of formal, statistically based, cognitive analysis is beyond the scope of this book. However, the basic premise of the approach can be used less formally and applied in any conflict situation.

The premise is "human judgment. . .provides a prime source of conflict and that many, though not all, disagreements flow from the exercise of human judgment. Consequently, even if self-serving motives are eliminated, interpersonal conflict will persist. Research. . .has indicated that, unaided a person faces difficulties in clarifying his or her judgment" (Al-tabtabai et al., 2001). In other words, people find it difficult to express the underlying reasons why they are for or against their position.

Cognitive analysis helps the parties to better understand why they have the positions they hold and this gives them greater ability to find win-win resolutions. The formal approach involves surveying key parties to the conflict regarding their specific values as represented in a number of hypothetical resolution possibilities. The results are statistically analyzed to determine the factors that led each party to their judgment regarding the case, resulting in a relative weight of importance to each party of each factor. Cognitive feedback from the analysis uncovers judgment agreements and differences. The differences are the basis for a highly focused negotiation process to see how differences can be reconciled.

This formal, statistical analysis is clearly overkill for the typical project dispute and is used in complex and important conflicts where there is the time and expertise required to engage the parties and do the analysis. However, the concept of exploring why each party holds his or her opinion is very applicable to any conflict.

The evaporating clouds conflict diagramming technique below uses a simplified cognitive approach to identify the underlying reasons for each party's position. The weights and scores decision-making approach, discussed in the chapter on Technique represents a simplified cognitive analysis.

Diagramming the Conflict—Evaporating Clouds

In *Thinking for a Change*, Lisa Scheinkopf (1999) quoted Aristotle: *"When we deliberate it is about means and not ends."* She points out that in her experience "every problem that exists can be described as a conflict in the form of an evaporating cloud" (p. 171). The conflict dissolves as you understand your own and the other parties' reasons and assumptions for their positions (Aristotle's means) and by identifying mutual objectives (the ends).

Conflict diagramming (Scheinkopf, 1999, pp. 171–191) is a cognitive analysis technique that helps the participants define their initial positions and discover the assumptions underlying them, their needs, shared common objectives and alternative solutions that satisfy the parties' needs, and their mutual objectives.

Figure 7-1 is an example. In it, a manager and a delivery team in a project are in conflict about how to address a particular project.

The manager is pushing for a low cost, rapid completion approach. The delivery team is pushing for an approach that will take longer and cost more but will more effectively (in their opinion) address long-term needs.

Using this diagramming technique the parties would go beyond just stating their demands. They must answer the question "Why do you want that?" to fill their needs boxes.

They fill in the mutual objectives box by collaboratively thinking of the bigger picture. They answer questions like "Is there a goal or objective that you share that would be satisfied by a win-win solution?" In this example, both can agree upon the goal of a satisfied client and sponsor, where the client is interested in an optimal solution for his problem and the sponsor is seeking a profit and repeat business.

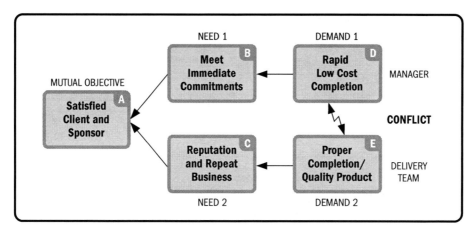

Figure 7.1: Diagramming a Conflict

Next, in the spirit of exploring mental models and taking a cognitive approach, each party explains the assumptions that led them to their perceived need and the assumptions that make them think that their demand will fill it. In this example, the manager assumes that it is his job to make sure the initial commitments made to the client for delivery within a set time frame must be met in order to satisfy the mutual objective—the company makes a profit and the client gets what he contracted for.

The delivery team assumes that the client is going to be dissatisfied if the time and cost constraints are met at the expense of quality, even though some of the quality attributes (for example the ability to change things about the product easily long after the project is over) were not spelled out in the contract.

With these assumptions on the table, the parties can explore the facts of the matter, past experiences, the expectations, and values of the client and sponsor, and ways of satisfying the needs of the parties and the objective. If this technique is used correctly and the parties are open to a mutually beneficial resolution the resolution may not look like either of the original demands.

If they cannot come to a resolution themselves, they will have sufficient information to present their cases to a higher authority.

Diversity—Cultural Differences

In addition to an analysis of mental models, cultural influences have to be assessed as these are often the source of conflict style preferences and behaviors and of reactions in conflict situations.

As a project manager, or in any role, your ability to work with others depends to a large degree on your understanding and acceptance of cultural differences and the way they influence behavior and relationships.

Frames and mental models are often the result of cultural conditioning and often include perceptions about others based on attributes like country of origin, age, and gender. Cultural intelligence (the ability to understand and work with one's own and other people's cultural tendencies) enables a conflict manager to manage diversity and thereby avoid unnecessary conflicts and more easily resolve the others.

The following discussion describes cultural traits that influence conflict management approach. As you read them, think of how it applies to your situations.

Culture

Culture is "the collective programming of the mind that distinguishes the members of one group or category of people from another" (Hofstede & Geert, 2005, p. 400). Culture implants deeply ingrained mental models. People identify themselves with their cultural traits. Cultural conditioning strongly influences behavior.

Hofstede and Geerte (2005, p. 400) analyzed cultural traits to identify five universal dimensions:

Power distance—social inequality and the relationship with authority;

Differences between collectivist and individualistic cultures—the relationships between individuals and their groups;

Concepts of femininity and masculinity—the perceived differences between them;

Uncertainty avoidance—how uncertainty is viewed and handled; and

Short-term vs. long-term orientation—focus on the future vs. focus on the present and past.

When working with people from different cultures, be aware of the cultural influence on their behavior. Be aware of your own tendencies and how they have been formed because of cultural conditioning. Adapt to the needs of the situation. Within reason and without violating your principles and values, accommodate to the other party's norms.

Following is a summary of how these five dimensions can influence conflict styles.

For a discussion of how different, nationality-based cultures map to the five dimensions see the Hofstede and Geert book, *Cultures and Organizations: Software of the Mind.*

Power Distance

Power distance is a measure of the degree to which members of a groups accept that power is distributed unequally. Where power distance is high, there is a great respect or fear for authority and position. Where power distance is low, the expectations are that those in authority positions act as servant-leaders and that they are just people in high positions. Where power distance is low, consultative decision making is a norm and there is an ease of being able to confront one's superiors. Where power distance is high, people may be afraid to confront their bosses or others in perceived authority positions. This affects conflict. Avoidance can become a norm unless those in authority actively promote confrontation and negotiation. Where people are from different cultures, consciously managing the difference and its effects becomes even more important.

Example: Let's revisit Amir and the centralization project described in the previous chapter on style and approach. Imagine if Amir had a collaborative style. He wanted and expected pushback and discussion between himself and his subordinates to come to a consensus about how best to proceed. And, imagine that he is operating in a culture in which there was a very high power distance in which subordinates felt that it was disrespectful to disagree or question the boss or they feared that if they did question the boss they might be at personal risk. If Amir assesses the cultural and other factors that might influence the way he and his team interact, he will be more likely to promote the healthy conflict that he desires.

In this scenario, Amir opts to ask his team to first decide whether creating a high degree of consistency among the branches would be beneficial and if it was, to identify two or three alternative ways to do it. Amir makes sure that one of the alternatives is the one he likes, though he does it without expressing his preference. He sets some reasonable time constraint and expectations regarding level of detail in the analysis.

Here, the end result will be a choice among (1) leaving things as they are; (2) changing them by instituting a degree of consistency while allowing for individual branch styles; or (3) instituting complete consistency. The approach and which vendors to use will depend on the outcome of this choice.

Without conflict among Amir's subordinates, the chances of finding, implementing and sustaining a process that satisfies the organizations needs are low. Seeing this, Amir uses his understanding to lead his team into healthy conflict and resolution. He stays on the sidelines until late in the process.

Note the gamesmanship at play. Amir is subtly influencing the group. Is he trying to put something over on them to their detriment or is he trying to get an optimal result that will benefit the group and the stakeholders around it? Also, note that in some cultures, Amir coming to the group for an answer might be perceived as a weakness. His subordinates might think that it is the boss' job to decide.

Amir might go another step towards collaboration by bringing the power distance issue to the group's attention and showing the group how the process he is guiding them through addresses it without violating any cultural values. He can do this before addressing the content, during the conflict, as issues arise or after it has been resolved, depending on the needs of the situation. This approach brings mental models and cultural issues to light and has the power to change the overall conflict management process rather than just resolving the conflict at hand.

Collectivist vs. Individualistic

In collectivist cultures, the interest of the group prevails over the interest of the individual. People more strongly identify with the group as opposed to themselves as individuals. The group may be a family, extended family, community, company, department, or team. Harmonizing, conforming to the group, commitment to group goals and values, and maintaining "face" (respect in the eyes of the group) are highly valued. People from collectivist cultures tend to be higher on the cooperativeness scale and lower on the assertiveness scale than people in individualistic cultures.

In individualistic cultures, there is a high value on autonomy, independence, personal creativity, personal growth, and personal time. "I" am at the center of things.

> Individualists and collectivists view conflict differently. Collectivists often see conflict as a sign of social failure. As a result, people are less comfortable with conflict situations, especially of an interpersonal nature. Conflict is often avoided. While many individualists also feel discomfort with conflict, it is more likely to be acknowledged as an inevitable part of life that must be dealt with. In collectivist cultures, mediators are often expected to provide counsel, evaluate and advise in an effort to restore harmony. Disputants engage a third party precisely because they are unable to find a solution themselves. (Ford, 2001)

Concepts of Femininity and Masculinity

In this dimension, we are not dealing with gender. Cultures as a whole tend towards one or the other poles on the feminine/masculine continuum. The Hofstede and Geert (2005) survey found that for the masculine pole earnings, recognition, advancement, and challenge were the highest valued, and at the feminine pole, good working relationships, cooperation, living area, and employment security were most highly valued. Femininity is associated with the cooperative scale in the conflict styles model while masculinity is associated with the assertiveness scale.

A *masculine* society is defined as one in which "emotional gender roles are clearly distinct: men are supposed to be assertive, tough, and focused on material success, whereas women are supposed to be more modest, tender, and concerned with the quality of life.

"A society is called *feminine* when emotional gender roles overlap: both men and women are supposed to be modest, tender and concerned with the quality of life" (Hofstede and Geert, 2005, p. 120).

When we analyze our conflict situations with these traits in mind we can better predict behavior and choose a style that is most likely to be effective. We can more clearly see when either over assertiveness or over concern for cooperative resolutions is operating to impact the quality of the solution. Are we being too accommodating; too assertive? Are we assuming that the other parties are as interested in collaboration as we are? How can we moderate our normal tendencies to better deal with the situation at hand?

Uncertainty and Ambiguity Tolerance

As we analyzed the nature of a conflict, we saw that degree of certainty and reversibility are attributes of a conflict. Uncertainty avoidance is a dimension of cultural identity that influences conflict management. There are individual and cultural levels of acceptable uncertainty and ambiguity. Too much ambiguity and there is intolerable anxiety. Where uncertainty avoidance is high we find a greater need for structure and a greater desire for authority based resolutions which are often irreversible. There is greater likelihood of compromises, conflict avoidance, and accommodation as means for addressing conflict when ambiguity tolerance is low.

Short-term vs. Long-term Orientation

This dimension addresses the degree to which people focus on the future vs. on the present and past. Long-term orientation values future rewards, whereas short-term orientation values virtues that relate to the past and present (Hofstede and Geert, 2005, p. 210).

Awareness of this dimension helps to explain and predict behavior that may cause people to take the positions they have in conflict situations. Someone who has a high degree of long-term orientation may be willing to sacrifice short-term harmony and order to achieve a future goal. This may create conflicts in a team where the traditional way of doing things is highly valued by some. At the same time, a long-term orientation may motivate giving up immediate rewards to cultivate good relations that will pay off in the future. Short-term orientation will seek quick effective solutions, but may not sufficiently assess long-term effects.

Systemic Change in Relationships

Addressing and changing mental models and the cultural influences that impact them is <u>not</u> easy. In many instances, it may be impossible. It often calls for a change in the relationships among the parties and their conflict management process.

As mental models are explored and become subject to change, systemic change or transformation can occur. Consciously managing the process increases the probability of a more effective resolution of individual disputes and sets the stage for a continuously improving way of operating.

If you have authority, your position makes it easier to convince others to take the time and effort to step back and take a cognitive approach. Without authority you might use your influence to promote a cognitive approach by asking questions like, "Do we really want to go through another round of failure or can we try to see if we can change things?" or "Can we work together more effectively if we take a more methodical and analytical approach?" Use history, the pains experienced, and the positive experiences, to justify improvement to the conflict management process. Perhaps you can request training in conflict management or diversity awareness or mindfulness or integrate these into a facilitated kick-off session for your project.

At the same time, don't get caught up in an idealistic quest to change your organization's culture that takes you away from the focus on your current project and conflict. As a project manager, your project is your primary responsibility. Stepping back to understand yourself and the other people involved, their styles, motivations, etc., will enable you to be more effective.

Chapter Summary

Seeking to understand ourselves and others extends our analysis to the psychological/behavioral realm. It is not sufficient to know the attributes and characteristics of our conflicts. Assess conflict styles, mental models, diversity, and the effects of emotional intelligence to better understand yourself and the others. Better understanding strengthens your ability to manage any situation.

If a conflict arises and the parties have not yet explored styles, diversity and emotional intelligence, it is not too late. Facilitate a discussion of these factors and seek mutual understanding. Open dialogue, moderated by someone who has insight into interpersonal dynamics and the practical issues in play, provides the fertile ground needed to ensure that disputes and conflicts are managed in a healthy and productive way. Motivate this type of discussion by highlighting how chronic problems and patterns get in the way of effective solutions and how they are caused by interpersonal and intrapersonal issues.

At the same time, avoid overdoing it. Don't get too "touchy feely." Assess the readiness of your group and work accordingly. Cultivate the facilitation techniques, discussed in the next chapter, and the sensitivity that comes with heightened mindfulness to apply a cognitive approach.

Emotional intelligence is perhaps the most important personal attribute to cultivate. It is what enables responsiveness and responsiveness enables effective conflict management.

Mindfulness or the underlying capability of being consciously aware of thoughts and feelings as they arise is an essential capability that can be cultivated using insight meditation. It is essential because it enables emotional intelligence and the self-management that goes along with it.

Chapter 8

Facilitate Rapport

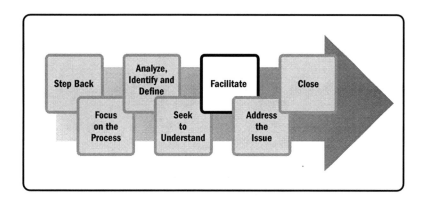

Chapter Overview

The previous chapters have focused on gathering information about the process, the conflict, and the people. In this chapter, the emphasis shifts from knowing to doing.

While we have addressed some techniques (e.g., mindfulness meditation and communications planning), up until this point we have focused on what you need to know to effectively manage conflict. In this chapter and the one following, we focus primarily on techniques that apply the principles and values we have explored and make use of the knowledge that has come out of the analysis.

This chapter addresses facilitation and mediation and the way they can be integrated into the conflict management process to enable the parties to collaborate to address the conflict. In order to most effectively address the content issues, engender a relationship among the parties that allows practical, open, and collaborative communication.

Rapport

One of the critical skills in a conflict manager's toolkit is cultivating rapport with and among the other parties. Rapport is a relationship of mutual trust, emotional affinity, similarity, and common interests. It is associated with conformity, accord and correspondence.

Clearly, rapport is a key ingredient when addressing conflict. The greater the rapport, the more likely it is that the parties can avoid reactivity driven by fear or mistrust. Rapport is created via communication, both verbal and non-verbal, among the parties. It is influenced by values such as openness and win-win attitudes.

To facilitate rapport you need to be mindfully aware of what is going on in and around you so you can help set everyone else at ease and make sure they focus on the content.

You do not need to be a professional facilitator or mediator to help to create rapport. Every participant should cultivate trust and avoid the unnecessary impact of anger, fear, and greed. Create an environment in which everyone can say their piece, feel as if they have been heard and stay on target. These methods set the stage for negotiation, dialogue, and debate, to be discussed in the next chapter.

The sections following explore facilitation and mediation and their place in conflict management.

Facilitation/Mediation

Facilitators and mediators (we will use the terms interchangeably) don't have the authority to settle a dispute. They help to ensure that the conflicting parties engage in an effective process, stepping back, analyzing, and understanding their motivations and the motivations of others. They facilitate readiness to engage and address the issue at hand for closure. On a subtle level, the mediator influences the conflicting parties by being present in a calm, objective, focused, energized, and peaceful way. This presence is contagious, affecting the way people feel and respond to one another.

Facilitators or mediators may limit their scope to the communication/relationship process or give advice, influence outcomes or offer information.

Facilitation is not just for communication professionals and academics. As a project manager, supervisor or functional manager, parent, friend, etc., you will be called upon to help others resolve conflicts. As a party to a conflict you can also facilitate to keep communication open, avoid emotionality and keep to the topic and within an agreed upon conflict management process.

Mediation and Mindfulness

Earlier we introduced mindfulness meditation. Mediation and meditation, according to the *Online Etymology Dictionary*, share the same root, 'med' mind, to think about, measure, moderate, judge, limit, consider, advise. Mediation is to intervene between two parties, to facilitate.

Facilitators must take a step back to be mindfully aware and calm in order to apply their skills. They must be highly responsive and non-reactive. They should exude a sense of calm competent presence that is transferred to the others in the group so the group can perform optimally.

Here is what one expert has to say about the need to apply mindfulness to the task of mediation. The approach is equally important for anyone involved in conflict.

> We can become aware of our habitual ways of conducting ourselves in mediation so that before we act we can notice our impulse to act, and decide whether or not to carry through on the impulse. So, for example, if a client begins to raise his voice and the mediator begins to feel anxiety, the mediator's normal reaction might be to insist that the client lower his voice. However, if you are really mindful, you can notice the anxiety come up and the impulse to quiet the client. Based on this awareness, you would be able to decide whether you want to carry through on the impulse to quiet the client or decide to release your own anxiety. In other words, if you are aware of the anxiety, sometimes that awareness without judgment is enough to cause the anxiety to dissipate and to have less power over you so that you are able to decide to let it be. Similarly, you could do the same thing with your impulse to react in a certain way. (Lazarus, 2005).

With awareness, you can decide how to act and to not react. For example, as a mediator you want to clearly show understanding as opposed to agreement. It is a well-known guideline in facilitation to be careful of nodding or saying "yes" when you mean "I understand." Awareness comes into play as you consciously decide to notice whether you nod and how you signal understanding as opposed to agreement.

Maintaining Concentrated Awareness

Awareness implies a degree of concentration, the ability to remain focused on a chosen point of reference, for example, the proceedings in a meeting, the content and demeanor of other parties' communication, your feelings and behavior, etc. Being relaxed and concentrated brings on a sense of being calm and centered.

To enhance your concentration, try this practice: simply choose a point of attention (it can be your breath, a sound, word or phrase, the sensations of your body, a task, the content of a meeting, etc.), notice when you are becoming or have become distracted and then, if you have become distracted, gently but firmly, bring your attention back to the point. Keep bringing your attention back to your reference point. Be patient with yourself; the mind naturally wanders.

Doing this practice over and over again strengthens concentration and, if done in a formal sitting. brings on states of calm quiet relaxation.

Techniques for Building Rapport

The point of cultivating and using your concentration and awareness is so that you can perform more effectively as a conflict manager. Concentration and awareness are the foundation for the techniques discussed below. These techniques are focused on setting people at ease and making sure that they communicate effectively.

There is a circular relationship—you need to be aware and to concentrate to apply the techniques while applying the techniques strengthens your awareness and concentration. You do not have to believe that just because I have said so. Do an experiment. Like with everything in this book, try it, and see if it works.

The following sections explore six facilitation techniques that enable effective conflict management. They are:

1. Active listening—taking the effort to hear and understand what others are saying;
2. Questioning—enabling active listening by digging into the other parties communication and making sure your understanding is accurate;
3. Matching and mirroring—creating a sense of trust and comfort;
4. Using body language—going beyond the words;
5. Making eye contact—maintaining trust and comfort; and
6. Moderating the communication process—managing the flow of communication.

Setting People at Ease

When you are comfortably relaxed, alert, supported with the right tools and work environment, trusting and respectful of the people you are with, is performance better or worse than when there is animosity and emotionality, unnecessary stress or discomfort? Perhaps this is a dumb question; though if the answer is obvious, are you doing what is needed to cultivate performance enhancing "ease."

The first five techniques set people at ease to build rapport while the sixth incorporates these five to keep the parties on target to address the conflict content.

Facilitation techniques are "background tasks." They are subtly applied as you dialogue, negotiate, and debate, whether you are one of the parties or an outside facilitator/mediator. The techniques require training and practice as well as concentrated attention to your own and/or other people's behavior and feelings. While they need to be cultivated, many people use them naturally. A master conflict manager has integrated these into his process.

Skillfulness and Intention

Be careful. If your purpose is building rapport and trust, then you want to be very subtle and skillful in the way you use facilitation techniques.

You have most probably experienced the sense that you are being manipulated or played in some way. Maybe it was an overly assertive sales person or someone on a help desk or an overly solicitous hotel service employee or headwaiter. Did it make for more or less rapport? Did it make you feel more or less open?

Generally, the more your intention is to seek a win-win solution the easier it is to reach rapport. You naturally behave and speak in a way that is a reflection of your intention. If the other party senses that you are trying to manipulate them they will likely close down. Even if your intention was positive, you will lose trust. Lose trust and rapport is gone; openness is gone.

To master the techniques, 'play' with them in a relatively safe environment; see if they work and how good you are at using them before using them in a critical conflict situation.

Active Listening

Active listening means paying strict attention to all speakers, asking appropriate questions for clarity, and double-checking understanding. It lets the parties know that they have been heard and understood. Active listening also helps the speaker hear what she is saying and how it is being understood. It helps the listener to stay focused on what is being said, both verbally and non-verbally and it helps the listener know whether he has understood what has been said in the way the speaker meant it to be understood.

Sometimes just articulating the parties' arguments or positions is all that is needed to resolve a conflict. Sometimes it clarifies that there really is no conflict at all, only a misunderstanding because of miscommunication.

Listening goes beyond the content of the discussion and it is not limited to the use of the ears. Being aware of the other party requires hearing, seeing, and feeling. Listen to notice changes in tone, and word usage as well as content. Observe visual cues such as shifts in posture, facial expressions, where their eyes are focused, glances shared between them and others present. Allow the natural capacity of the right brain to do its job to recognize and interpret facial expressions and the whole picture.

Listen to yourself as well as to the other people.

"Listen" to your feelings—the sensations in the body that inform you of subtle reactions to current circumstances. Do you feel comfortable or threatened? Does a particular thing the other party says or does trigger a physical reaction in your gut or chest or throat? Is the feeling positive or negative? How does it make you want to behave?" Awareness of your own feelings enables you to reduce the probability of reactive behavior.

Here are some listening tips:

Pay attention. If you find that your thoughts get in the way, practice insight meditation or another technique to improve your awareness and concentration. Active listening promotes mindfulness and concentration in both the listener and speaker.

Don't show frustration or amusement even when others are behaving in ways that may cause it to arise. Displaying these feelings will often result in the other party pulling away and possibly magnify the behavior you are reacting to.

Maintain eye contact while avoiding an unnatural "eye-lock" or anything that would make the speaker uncomfortable. There are cultural and individual differences regarding eye contact so be careful and explore every one's norms so you can behave in a way that engenders trust and ease of communication

Summarize, restate, or rephrase what you hear to validate your understanding and show that you are engaged and paying attention. Be mindful of overdoing it. When the issues are complex or there is need for documentation, take notes that can be seen by everyone using flip chart, white board, or electronic media. Putting the recap down in writing enables a more effective analysis of the content and leaves documentation. People tend to be more precise in their thinking and communication when the results are being put in writing.

Go beyond the words to perceive body language, tone of voice and other emotional cues; if situationally appropriate, bring the insights from these cues to the attention of the parties so they can be more self-reflective and aware of the subtleties that they may be missing.

Avoid confrontations with participants that would embarrass them in front of the group or take the group into a focus on 'process' when they need to be resolving the issue at hand.

Questioning

Questioning is a key technique in active listening. The ability to ask questions in a way that engages the other party in a discovery process enables the parties to get a clear sense of what is happening, what the cause of their conflict is, what their needs and wants are, and what is needed to resolve the conflict and/or avoid future conflicts.

Questioning is also a way to get the other party to say things that bring out points you would rather they make. When one says something, he or she tends to "own" it more so than if they hear someone else say it.

Imagine how you would feel if someone said to you, "What you are doing is really making other people angry." How would you feel and what would you say if someone asked, "What do you think the others are feeling when you fail to respond to their emails?"

Avoid loaded or leading questions to manipulate the other parties. For example, rather than asking "Don't you think that what you are asking for is unreasonable, given the other parties situation and needs?" you might ask, "How do you think the other party will respond to what you are asking for?"

Facilitation styles that resemble the cross examination of a hostile witness tend to engender distrust and resistance. Closed questions with single answers (yes or no, this or that) may make people feel hemmed in and confronted. This may lead them to lose trust in the process and withdraw into their position.

Of course, closed questions can be used to be sure that answers are understood. You might ask "Do I understand you correctly, that you find the design feature proposed by Jim acceptable for inclusion in the new product?" This is a yes or no question but it leaves the other person with an alternative to equivocate.

In general, though, ask open-ended questions. Elicit information to enable reflection on causes, effects, feelings, wants, needs and possible solutions. Open questions invite people to say what they really think and know. Here are some examples of effective open-ended questions (Ramsey, 1996, pp. 6–7):

How do you feel about—?

Why?

What do you mean?

"What if—?

Explain more about—.

What do you think about—?

How would you change things?

What do you want to happen?

What's causing the problem?

Can you elaborate on—?

What's the best case scenario? Tell me more about—?"

Matching and Mirroring

People often unconsciously recognize similarities and differences between the way they and others behave, speak, appear, move, sit and stand. Likeness breeds comfort and trust making for greater ease among people.

In neuro-linguistic programming (NLP), mirroring and matching are techniques that help to gain rapport on an unconscious level. As people work or socialize together, they tend to synchronize their behavior, a collective style emerges. Recognizing this, one can make the other party or parties feel comfortable by mirroring and matching their behavior.

For example, if people wear a shirt, tie, and jacket to every meeting, you might decide to dress like the others. The theory being that you will be more easily perceived as one of the group. Of course, there may be good reason for you to not want to be perceived as one of the group; perhaps you want to highlight a difference to make a point or set a tone.

On a more subtle level, you can mirror or match tone of voice, posture, blinking, breathing, facial expressions, gestures, and word usage.

You can take a mirror image posture. If the other person is sitting with his left elbow on the table and is leaning left, you might take a similar posture with your right elbow on the table.

Listen to the speed of their speech, their style, how they approach a sentence, their tone, what is important to them personally, their way of dressing, their posture. If they use the term "see" to connote understanding or awareness, as in "Oh, I see!" or "How do you see it?", then you can start using the same term rather than something like "I get it" or "I understand." Similarly are they using "feel" to mean "I believe" or "I think."

Note how I used the word "listen" to have a broader meaning than the typical definition connotes. If there is the sense that the use of a word in that way disturbs the other party, then shift and become more literal. Be aware of the metaphors the other party is using. If they use sports metaphors, you might choose to adopt them as well.

For example, if the other party says something like "Let's shoot for lots of singles instead of a home run." You might respond with "Yes, consistent hitting keeps us on base and in the end we'll win with less risk." instead of "We need to take an incremental approach with lots of quick wins."

Of course, if you are into football, knitting, reading, skiing, cricket, or rugby and know nothing about baseball and therefore have no idea what the other person is talking about, you might ask that person to explain. In that way you open to them by admitting your ignorance and creating rapport because you may both find that you share an interest in team sports and can relate on that level even though you don't know the same sport. You also avoid looking like a phony or a fool if you make believe you know what the other person means and that person discovers that you don't.

You can mirror incongruities like the use of a word like "great" to mean terrible, as in, "That's just great!" said with a downtrodden or angry tone or demeanor. You can use the term in a similar way to create rapport.

No one thing will really do the trick; it is the total affect that elicits the response. Remain aware of incongruence between your behavior and the behavior of the others and judiciously mirror their behavior to put them more at ease.

Body Language

Reading body language is part of active listening. Using body language is part of mirroring. Note the interplay between words and behavior, including facial expressions, gestures and body postures. It is said that word content accounts for less than 50 percent of the influence in communication. Some say that only 7 percent to 10 percent of conversation is verbal. The rest is non-verbal. Body language is non-verbal communication that consists of tone of voice, diction, posture, eye contact, and general affect. While body language is difficult to control, we can have some control and we can also use our knowledge of it to make for better communication as we negotiate our way to win-win resolutions.

Some people are really good at manipulating their body language to mask their feelings others just let it all hang out. In any case, there are what poker players called "tells"—subtle clues to what the other party is experiencing. Only masters are adept at truly hiding their feelings. Most of the people we deal with are not masters of their body language.

Reading body language is a bit of an art. A right-brain activity takes the whole into account rather than trying to discern each part of the posture to build an impression analytically. It requires mindfulness and relaxed concentration.

Body posture both influences our 'energy' and is influenced by it. Note the difference between the way you feel when you are slumped over with your shoulders rolled forward, your head and neck hanging down, and your face in a frown versus the way you feel when you are comfortably erect with your head and neck in a line, chin slightly tucked, shoulders rolled back and down and a gentle smile on your lips.

Try each posture for a couple of minutes or so and experience the difference.

You can control the way you feel by the way you sit, stand, and move around. If you are beginning to feel angry or defensive or fearful, try changing your posture so that you are more erect and your chest is open. Rather than painting a phony smile on your face, smile warmly to yourself. You might visualize a smile taking form in the back of your head. Let an inner smile naturally change your facial expression.

Even if you do not have visual contact with the other parties, be aware of your posture and body language. Some people use a mirror to inform them of how they are looking so they can more easily read and adjust their posture to elicit positive feelings and overcome tiredness and boredom.

When you are face to face, you can go beyond mirroring and matching to influence the other party. Once you have mirrored their posture, say, a slouch, change your posture. As you straighten up you may find them changing their posture to match yours.

Be aware of body language and of your natural ability to read it, almost unconsciously. Trust your ability to interpret the non-verbal cues while being aware that there are cultural and other factors at play that may have one posture or gesture mean different things to different people.

Being aware of and in control of your body language and being aware of the body language of the others informs your approach.

Eye Contact

As you are engaged with the other parties, using active listening, matching, and mirroring, aware of body language add eye contact as another part of putting people at ease while being in control of yourself and the situation.

An old proverb says "The eyes are the mirror of the soul." Our eyes express our feelings, moods, and attitudes more so than any other part of our body language. Making eye contact is a powerful way to show interest in the other person and in what they have to say and to communicate willingness to be open. A lack of eye contact is often interpreted as a sign of hiding something, lack of interest, disagreement or lying. We build rapport by being perceived as interested and open.

A simple technique is to make a note of a person's eye color when you meet them. It forces you to look them in the eye for a moment.

However, be aware that there are cultural and individual differences regarding eye contact. In some cultures where hierarchy and status are important looking a superior in the eye may be considered offensive. Shy people may avoid eye contact. As always, take the whole picture in to get a sense of the other person's responses and attitudes.

Keep in mind that eye contact does not mean some kind of eye lock. When the eye contact is prolonged and intense it may be interpreted as being a sign of aggression or as a sign of romantic interest. Be aware of how the other party is responding to your eye contact. Keep direct eye contacts brief and generally look at the other parties face without grabbing hold of their gaze with yours.

When you look into another person's eyes, your natural ability to read body language comes into play and you can often see much about the way they are feeling. Experts take this a step further by attempting to read subtle eye movements to determine whether what is being said is coming from imagination, factual knowledge, or deep memory. Clearly, this requires training, a lot of practice and great care to consider individual and other influences.

Moderating Communication

This technique skillfully uses listening, questioning and the other techniques. Moderating the communication process seeks to make it possible for each party to efficiently address the conflict while giving everyone the chance to be heard and understood. It builds rapport because it creates a safe and comfortable environment and keeps the parties on track by highlighting diversions as they arise.

As a facilitator, prepare yourself by making sure you know the subject and the group's goals. Prepare the group by discussing and getting agreement regarding the facilitator role and how the group members will communicate. Make sure that the parties are aware of the need for process awareness while they are managing their conflict.

Make sure that the group has an agenda and stays reasonably close to it as they address their issues. Make sure that shy people get an opportunity to speak and that the overly assertive do not monopolize the conversation. Promote fact-based decision making. Make sure that firm decisions are made with input from many voices. Use active listening and questioning.

If you are part of the group and there is no outside facilitator, you can apply the same approach, but it is more difficult. It is more difficult because you may find others to be resistant to your attempts to bring tangents back to the point of focus or when you address time issues or try to diffuse emotional issues.

It is a good practice to raise the facilitation issue and either appoint one of your group members as official facilitator or agree that the facilitation can be done informally by the members of the group. The important thing is to make sure the group is aware of facilitation.

Characteristics of a Facilitator

A facilitator or mediator applies the techniques we have discussed to build rapport, promote effective communication and to keep the parties on target. Ramsey (1996, pp. 5–6) provided the following list of the characteristics of an effective facilitator:

- Open-mindedness (no bias or pre-set opinions);
- Capacity to demonstrate empathy and sensitivity;
- Ability to accept all feelings as honest and valid;
- Willingness to allow disputants to own the problem and the solution;
- Flexibility and resiliency;
- Ability to remain calm;
- Objectivity and ability to depersonalize situations;
- Neutrality (avoid taking sides or jumping to conclusions);
- Patience and willingness to hear all sides without interruption;
- Sense of timing;
- Respect for confidentiality;
- Credibility and integrity;
- Ability to avoid trivializing anyone's opinion, values or feelings; and
- Unflinching commitment to stay on task

The list boils down to high emotional intelligence, open-minded objectivity, mindfulness, concentration, and process orientation. Note that even as a disputant, open-mindedness, objectivity, and neutrality are possible.

Remember, facilitation is not just for professional facilitators. Each party to a conflict can apply facilitation techniques to make it more likely that the participants achieve their goals. As a supervisor, functional manager, or project manager you will be very likely to face the inevitable conflicts in the course of work. You may be a subject matter expert but you also have a responsibility to <u>not</u> just make decisions as an authority but to facilitate agreement among the disputing parties, improve their ability to manage their own conflicts and share knowledge and experience. Don't rely on external facilitators/mediators (though in the right situation they are very valuable). You are it. Become an expert facilitator.

Chapter Summary

This chapter explored building rapport, facilitation, and mediation. Rapport is relationship in which there are mutual trust, emotional affinity, similarity, and common interests. Facilitation or mediation is a means for cultivating rapport and ensuring that there is a free and effective flow of communication among the parties towards addressing and resolving their conflict. Effective facilitation relies on the ability to be mindfully aware and focused in the midst of a conflict event. This sets the stage for you to choose the right techniques and apply them to keep the group on target and aware of its process.

If you are going to be involved in or managing others involved in conflict, learn to facilitate, not necessarily as a professional facilitator, but as one who can cultivate rapport without being manipulative.

That means learning the skills of active listening, questioning, mirroring, using body language and eye contact, and moderating the communication process.

Chapter 9

Approaches and Techniques

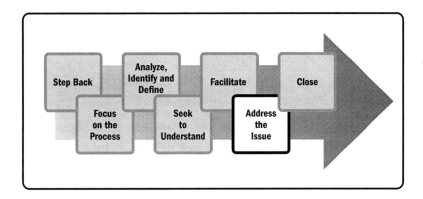

Chapter Overview

> *Seek an optimal resolution. Be mindful of reactive behavior and its long-term effects on relationships.*

In this chapter, we will explore the conflict management process step: *Address the Issue*. Dialogue, debate, decision-making/problem-solving, and negotiation are the core techniques used in addressing conflict issues.

The cognitive analysis approach to conflict management forms a foundation for the core techniques. We described evaporating cloud diagramming earlier as a means to help the parties *dissolve* the conflict as they clarify their positions, wants, needs, and mutual objectives so they can understand differences in judgment and areas of agreement. This approach is used within dialogue, debate, and negotiation.

Remember, resolution is not the only objective in conflict management. Some conflicts will not be resolved. The parties may agree to disagree and move forward, if it is possible, without obtaining agreement regarding content. We will discuss closure techniques, escalation, mediation, and arbitration, in the next chapter.

As you read about the techniques in this chapter, consider factors such as values, place in the project lifecycle, conflict type or cause, conflict attributes as well as the nature of the people involved and their environment. With this in mind, choose the techniques that are situationally appropriate. It will most likely be a hybrid approach that blends techniques.

Dialogue, Debate, Decision Making, and Negotiation

Dialogue, debate, decision making and negotiation are the predominant techniques used in conflict management. While they are each a distinct technique they may be used together within the same conflict. For example, once a conflict is acknowledged there can be

- a dialogue about it;
- an analysis of the conflict;
- debates over the subject—plans, designs, requirements, etc.;
- negotiation informed by the results of the dialogue and debate; and
- arbitration, mediation, or facilitation as needed.

Decision-making/problem-solving techniques may be used throughout the process.

We will explore dialogue, debate, decision making and negotiation in the following sections of this chapter.

Dialogue

"Dialogue is shared exploration towards greater understanding, connection or possibility" (Dialogue, n.d.a). It is divergent thinking—"thinking that moves away in diverging directions so as to involve a variety of aspects and which sometimes leads to novel ideas and solutions; associated with creativity." Conversely, convergent thinking is "thinking that brings together information focused on solving a problem (especially solving problems that have a single correct solution)" (Dialogue, n.d.b). The danger of convergent thinking is that it may ignore possibilities by inhibiting tangents. Its power is in the ability to get to a conclusion.

Dialogue is a communication process for achieving mutual understanding. William Isaacs, in *The Fifth Discipline Fieldbook*, tells us that dialogue won't work if it is done with the intent of making a decision. The reason is that intent will cut off the free flow of inquiry. It is the flow of inquiry that is the objective of dialogue.

What! No Conclusion?

The idea of engaging in a dialogue without the need for a decision or conclusion is frightening to many project managers. Time is usually a critical factor and open-ended dialogue may seem a luxury or even a waste of valuable time. In project situations, you need to balance convergent and divergent approaches. You take an act of faith in the power of dialogue, moderated by the practicality of cutting off dialogue at the right time; often the manager makes a judgment call that there has been sufficient sharing and exploring, given time, cost and quality constraints.

The power of dialogue

In its ideal form, dialogue can be magical. It can result in dissolving boundaries and opening up possibilities that were hidden from the parties. David Bohm (1996), the quantum physicist, defined Bohmian Dialogue. It is based on the idea that constructive thought is made possible through collective culture and conversation.

He noted that the word "discussion" comes from a root that connotes striking and shaking, like "percussion" and "concussion." You say this, I say that in response as if we were playing ping-pong. It is more like debate. Dialogue, on the other hand connotes joining and being involved in a shared pool of meaning within a fluid process. The process enables a level of understanding that could not be foreseen by the participants as individuals.

Tips for Dialogue

- Sit in a circle, an arrangement that doesn't favor anyone.
- Define the subject and objectives.
- Explain the ground rules—open communication to explore and understand as opposed to convince; meeting facilitation communication guidelines
- In principle, there is no need for a leader or facilitator or an agenda. However, the process is adaptive. A facilitator may be very useful, particularly in settings where everyone interrupts everyone else and there are multiple conversations going on all at once. The facilitator helps to get the group going, moderate communication, reflect on what is going and transfer facilitation skills to the members of the group.
- Promote and practice mindful observation of what is happening inside of you and in the dialogue you are part of. In Bohmian Dialogue, individuals explore any feelings that arise, including anxiety caused by having an open process and the fear of never reaching an end. Managing arising feelings is mostly an intrapersonal issue, though in some dialogues there is a sharing regarding feelings. Don't cut off discussion about feelings but also be careful not to let the dialogue turn into a group therapy session, unless that is what you want it to be. In the ideal, the dialogue is allowed to flow wherever it goes. In projects and business settings, some constraints on time and topic are practical as long as there is room for true dialogue.
- Take note of your typical style and adapt to the needs of the situation
- Make sure the group members are open to the possibility of upsetting others and being upset by them. Bohm says that small groups tend to easily and naturally come to a "cozy adjustment." People are too polite and tend toward avoiding conflict within the dialogue.

- Take notes. Information is flowing, agreements and disagreements are coming up, and details are being identified and discussed. This information can be very useful as the group begins to converge on a resolution.
- Let formal dialogue inform the way you regularly communicate to practice informal dialogue.

Recap: Dialogue

Dialogue is a divergent thinking technique for stepping back from positions and preconceived models to openly discuss an issue from multiple perspectives without trying to accomplish anything but mutual understanding. It is a way for unifying the parties and getting information to flow. Mindfulness is applied to monitor and work with arising feelings and how they affect the exchange of ideas. Dialogue is informed by the results of the analysis and often precedes debate and negotiation. Problem solving and decision making may be applied during dialogue.

Debate

Debate is the process of arguing your point and refuting others' points; it is considering or thinking about something carefully; to engage in an argument by discussing opposing points; it is to consider something; deliberate. To some to debate means to fight or quarrel.

Where dialogue is divergent thinking, debate is convergent. It seeks an end. In a formal debate, there is a winner and a loser. In a political debate, there should be an intention to get to the truth but also to persuade others that your way is the right way. In debate, we have proponents and opponents.

Debate may be formal or informal. With formal debate, the subject is established and the debaters face one another in the presence of judges who score the sides and declare a winner; there are stated rules. In projects, competing suppliers or teams may engage in more or less formal debate, for example, bidding contests in which vendors are invited to square off against one another to convince the judges (the buyer's decision makers) that they are the best choice.

In informal debate the parties face one another over a "real" conflict instead of one contrived by the leadership of the debate society. Informal debate is an integral part of conflict management. When done in a way that maintains good relationships and stays focused on facts and logic it is a critical step towards achieving resolution, often alongside dialogue and negotiation.

Argument

Debate combines logic, fact, and rhetoric (persuasion). The framework or context of the argument – the way the question is posed and the setting itself—and the demeanor of the participants significantly impact the outcome. Situational management, understanding the people, and content, being mindfully present, concentrated, open minded, and emotionally intelligent all come into play.

Logical argument examines the degree to which arguments are consistent with an axiom—a proposition that the parties consider to be self-evident and take for granted as truth. The argument that is most logical (consistent with the axiom) wins. For example, if the axiom is "short is best" then a logical argument would be based on it— "our way will take less time than theirs, because. . .."

Factual argument only examines the facts. It is characterized by objectivity, asking questions, deep investigation of details and proofs, using the information available and seeking out information that is missing.

Rhetoric is the art of speaking or writing effectively. It appeals to the emotions. There may be an association with insincerity. Rhetoric uses logical and factual argument along with techniques that elicit the emotions and moral thinking of the audience, judges, or whomever the speaker is seeking to persuade.

Rebuttal

In formal debate, each team presents its arguments and criticizes or rebuts the arguments of the opposition. We do the same thing in informal debates, where the presentations and rebuttals occur in a fluid conversation.

When rebutting another person's argument there is a need to apply logic, "Why is the argument wrong? What facts and examples support the rebuttal?"

Criticize the argument, not the speaker. Ridiculing the opponent or bringing up irrelevant issues do not address whether the content of what was said is right or wrong. As conflicts become heated and we enter into debate it is easy to forget that part of the goal is to maintain healthy relationships and end with an optimal resolution, even if it isn't yours.

Asking Questions

Questioning is one of the facilitation skills discussed in the chapter on facilitating rapport. It is often useful to state rebuttals in the form of questions rather than statements. In formal debate, you answer them yourself. In informal debates, you may get the opponent to answer, but always have your "right" answer in mind so you can bring out your point.

For example, when an opponent has described his position as "This way of getting the job done has worked many times before and will work this time" You might say "No it won't because. . ." Or you could choose to pose questions like "How close is our current situation to the ones in which the approach you propose worked?" "Is it true that in several cases similar to the one we have now there were some serious failures?"

In any case, debate is not a place for being shy and conflict avoidant. The objective is to look at the facts and create the kind of communication that leads to a conclusion.

Debating Skills

In the context of conflict management cultivate and apply debating skills:

- Know your objectives – Do you want to win at all cost or do you want to win and promote good will? What are the criteria that will be used to decide the result? Do the parties seek to use the debate as a step towards a win-win resolution or as a means for persuading a panel of judges or an arbitrator?
- Where does this debate fit in the grand scheme? Is it a minor part of a small part of a relatively small and insignificant project or is it central to the success of a major initiative?
- Know your subject matter – come prepared with the facts and an understanding of the logic. Arguments that state your position (for example, "X is true (or not) because of Y.") Solid facts and examples that both support and do not support your argument (if you fail to look at <u>all</u> of the facts you can be blindsided by your opponent). Assumptions or knowledge of your opposition's arguments, facts, and examples
- Know the rules of debate—explicit and tacit protocols—for example, is a formal slide show expected; are questions to be raised at any time or only as elicited by the speaker; is it acceptable for people to act emotionally, raising their voice, thumping the desk; is there a penalty for lying or making up facts and examples?
- Know your audience, judges, and opponents (the language they speak, their values and cultural norms, how they think and decide, etc.)
- Organize your presentation
  o How will you position your argument?
  o How will the main argument and its supporting arguments be related?
  o In what sequence will you order your arguments and examples to make the greatest impact? How will you adjust the sequence as the other party argues his side?
  o How will you tie your arguments and examples to the central question?
  o How will you rebut the opposition's arguments? What examples? What counter arguments?
  o How will you apportion your time?
- prepared for interruptions and surprises.
- Cultivate a natural style that is effective for the situation.

Styles of debate range from the desk pounding rant to the slow logical presentation. There is no one right way. Find an approach that you feel comfortable with and that fits the situation. Flex your style as needed.

These are some additional guidelines for debaters:

- Don't read your speech. Use notes to remind you of the content and the sequence.
- Don't show off your vocabulary. Speak in terms that can be easily understood by your audience
- Make eye contact.
- Use tone of voice and body language to reinforce your arguments and to cultivate passion, trust and respect.
- Avoid nervous habits.
- Create a balance between friendly informality and formality with its tendency to coldness.

Decision Making/Problem Solving

Decisions solve problems and resolve conflicts. Decisions may be to not resolve the issue or to resolve it in a specific way. In addition, there are many small decisions made throughout the conflict leading up to the final decision ranging from what the shape of the negotiation table should be to how best to respond to a question or comment. Decision-making skills greatly influence conflict management.

Decision making/problem solving is a process:

- Define the issue or question, its environment, and stakeholders;
- Agree upon decision criteria;
- Identify causes;
- Identify solution options;
- Analyze and compare solution options vis-à-vis the decision criteria;
- Decide;
- Take action—implement the decision;
- Monitor and adjust the outcome; and
- Reflect on the process for lessons learned.

Analytical knowledge, effective techniques, emotional intelligence, the skill, and knowledge of the decision makers and a focus on mutual objectives and win-win outcomes influence the decision and the ongoing relationships among the parties.

Decision-Making Principles

The following principles are applied across the decision-making process. They are obvious to some and perhaps new to others, either way, it is important to go into any conflict situation with a clear understanding of these principles:

- There are always trade-offs in complex decisions.
- There are often more than one 'right' ways.

- Consider what to do if you cannot come to a decision – escalation is discussed in the chapter on closure.
- Know the decision criteria – Decisions are always made based on criteria; sometimes the criteria are consciously known and sometimes they are not; sometimes they are rational, sometimes not.
- Assumptions may be explicit or tacit; they are usually present and need to be mutually understood and assessed for validity
- Hold off making the decision until the last moment; be open to as much information as possible upon which to base your decision.
- Consider the uncertainty and reversibility of the decision – analyze long and short term risk of decision alternatives on the project, the stakeholders and yourself.
- Consider the effect of the decision-making method (democratic, authoritarian, collaborative) and approach (intuitive, analytical).

Decision-Making Method: Consensus and Its Alternatives

Decisions are made in one of the following ways – consensus, majority, plurality, or authority. In general,

- Shoot for consensus, but
- Be ready for authority based decisions to manage time, cost, and decision quality
- Majority and plurality are the weakest way to make decisions in projects and organizations

Consensus is most associated with the collaborative conflict style. Consensus means that all of the parties agree with, accept, and support the resolution decision. Getting everyone to agree requires time and effort and generally leads to superior solutions. Dialogue, debate, negotiation, cognitive analysis, and facilitation/mediation are all applied to bring the parties to a consensus.

In the context of projects, time and effort are major factors. You (as a project manager or collectively as a team) must decide when to abandon the quest for consensus and rely on authority, majority, or plurality. These require less time and effort and are informed by the results of consensus process. In making this decision, consider the effect of a non-consensus decision on buy-in and the ability to implement the decision. Will people accept the authority or democratically reached solution and implement it? How will it affect future relationships and the quality of the solution?

Democratically reached decisions, in project situations, are generally weak. They leave a minority that has not agreed that the solution is a good one that does the job. Further, there is no correlation between the number of people in favor of something and the 'goodness' of that something. The majority may be wrong and without sufficient exploration towards achieving consensus you might not know it until it is too late to do anything about it.

Decision-Making Approaches: Intuitive and Analytical

Whether they are made by consensus or authority, there are two principle ways for making decisions – intuitively and analytically. The intuitive approach relies heavily on the experience and skill of the decision makers; it minimizes analysis. Analytical approaches take longer and rely on the use of information structured to identify facts, criteria and their relative priorities or weights. One way is not better than the other, and they should be used together to support and reinforce one another. The following sections explore each of them in more detail.

Intuitive Decision Making

Recognition-primed decision (RPD) is a model that describes a way people make quick and effective decisions in complex situations. In effect, the decision maker comes up with a possible course of action and compares it to constraints by imagining various scenarios and chooses the first option not to be rejected. It may not be the best option but it is one that is expected to work. This kind of decision making requires the decision makers to have solid experience in the subject at hand and in decision making.

Problems may arise because of the failure to fully assess long-term risk and to accurately assess the similarity of the current situation to the past situations that have informed the decision makers. Superior options may be missed.

Gut feel is another aspect of intuitive decision making. It can be argued that gut feel is the result of a very quick assessment of the situation as in RPD as opposed to some mystical creative power of intuition. Whatever it is, learn to both trust and question your 'gut'. In most conflict situations, there is some time to reflect. The more complex and important the issue, the more likely a structured, analytical approach using analytical methods is needed.

Blink responses (a term popularized by Malcolm Gladwell, 2005) can be and often are the right ones, but if there is time; use a combination of analysis and intuitive assessment.

Analytical Assessment: Weights and Scores

Analysis is a major theme throughout this book. We analyzed the conflict as an object and the nature of the content subject and people with their positions, needs, wants, etc. Analysis is the linear and hierarchical decomposition of a subject to obtain knowledge and insight into the object's nature.

Complex decisions are based on the analysis of an array of often-conflicting criteria. For example, when choosing a product, ease of use, overall quality, cost, time

Weights/ Alternatives	Criteria			Weighted Score
	Cost	Time to Completion	Quality	
Criteria Weights	0.2	0.15	0.4	
Design 1	25	20	15	7.5
Design 2	10	30	20	9.92
Design 3	30	10	30	12.96

Figure 9-1: Weights and Scores example

to market, the availability of support, and price are all criteria. The principles of cognitive analysis are applied to identify the criteria and their relative priorities and then use them to make the decision.

The weighted sum model (WSM) is a grid analysis or a weights and scores analysis. It is widely used and relatively simple. It evaluates alternatives across a number of decision criteria, representing strengths, benefits, weaknesses, penalty, or cost. We will use it here as an example of the analytical approach.

The technique is to first identify the criteria and their relative weights, identify the alternatives, score each alternative using a common scale and unit of measure, apply the weights to the scores and then sum the weighted scores to identify the alternative with the highest score (or lowest if the criteria are costs as opposed to benefits). Figure 9-1 shows an example. The scores are in common units that would be a relative cost, time, and quality rating.

There are variations that consider the relative scores between alternatives for each criterion and eliminate the need for a common unit of scoring.

Other Techniques

There are many other techniques for making decisions that involve quantifying multiple criteria or other approaches. Some require training, experienced facilitators and computer support. The following list (http://en.wikipedia.org/w/index.php?title= Special:Search&search=decision+making+techniques) is a good starting point for researching them:

Weighted product method (WPM)
Analytic hierarchy process (AHP)
Analytic network process (ANP)
Inner product of vectors (IPV)
Multi-attribute value theory (MAVT)
Multi-attribute utility theory (MAUT)
Multi-attribute global inference of quality (MAGIQ)

Goal programming
ELECTRE (outranking)
PROMETHÉE (Outranking)
Data envelopment analysis
The evidential reasoning approach
Dominance-based rough set approach (DRSA)
Aggregated indices randomization method (AIRM)
Nonstructural fuzzy decision support system (NSFDSS)
Grey relational analysis (GRA)
Superiority and inferiority ranking method (SIR method)
Potentially all pair-wise rankings of all possible alternatives (PAPRIKA)
Value engineering (VE)
Value analysis (VA)

Decisions by the Numbers?

The weights and scores and other methods force people to explicitly state and weight their criteria. But, don't make the mistake of thinking this is about just deciding by the numbers. Instead, use it to support informed decision making.

Adjust the definition of the criteria and their weights and the scores using what-if analysis; for example, "What if we say that cost is more or less important?" When the numbers show a clear winner and someone is still holding out they may have an unstated criteria. Bringing it to light helps to either remove the objection (say, if it was a personal preference) or add the criterion, which changes the numbers. This technique is used in negotiation and is a means to discover agreements and differences in judgment among the parties and then to work explicitly with them to achieve a relatively objective resolution. It is cognitive analysis in action. It sets the conflicting parties facing the conflict as opposed to one another.

Recap Decisions Making Methods

Intuitive decision making is quick and recognizes that in complex decisions there is no single answer and rarely enough time to completely analyze and explore the subject. Analytical decision making promotes the objectivity required to minimize emotionality, arbitrary decisions, and politics. It seeks to make sure decisions are made based on explicitly stated criteria and that the participants work together to address the problem and make a decision that will resolve the conflict.

Decisions may be made by consensus, majority, plurality, or authority. The choice depends on the situation.

Decision making/problem solving is integrated into dialogue, debate, and negotiation. It occurs across the project life cycle and throughout the conflict management process.

Negotiation

Negotiation is a discussion to reach agreement. It represents convergent thinking in that it seeks a conclusion. It is through negotiation that most project related conflicts are resolved. Negotiation uses the result of cognitive analysis, dialogue, decision making, and debate sessions in which the parties define and explore the issues.

The basic principles and techniques that apply to conflict management apply to negotiation. *Getting to Yes*, by Fisher and Ury (1981) is a must read for anyone wanting a classic book on how best to negotiate. The approach described by Fisher and Ury is based on the idea of reaching mutually acceptable agreement. They recommend the following method:

- Don't bargain over positions—Seek an understanding of motivations, interests, needs and common objectives.
- Separate people from the problem—Step back and focus the attention of the parties on the problem to collaboratively solve it.
- Invent options for mutual gain—creatively work out ways to achieve mutual objectives.
- Insist on using objective criteria to reach a conclusion—rely on facts and well founded assumptions to overcome anger, fear and power plays.
- Be prepared with a best alternative to a negotiated agreement (BATNA)—the action you would take if the conflict cannot be resolved in the form of a mutual agreement.

Seem familiar? These are the basic principles we have been discussing for conflict resolution: seek common objectives and win-win solutions, understand the difference between the relationship issues and the content, work together against the problem, and rely on facts. In effect, the same principles and techniques we have discussed apply to negotiation.

Recap: Approaches and Techniques

We recommend a hybrid approach that is based on cognitive analysis to make sure that you are aware of your own and the other parties' judgment criteria, positions, needs, wants and of mutual objectives.

Analysis of the conflict to determine its nature, defined process and an awareness of the people side provide the knowledge needed to come to a resolution, which may be to agree to not resolve the conflict.

The analysis itself may result in a resolution as the parties realize that they have no conflict or that they can easily resolve it by shifting their criteria and priorities. The evaporating cloud and weights and scores techniques, among others, apply cognitive analysis to make sure that rational criteria and mutual objectives are driving the process.

To get to a resolution, the parties dialogue, debate, apply decision-making techniques and negotiate. They combine intuitive and analytical approaches. They make sure they are cognizant of the long-term impact of their decisions and actions, applying emotional intelligence and facilitation techniques to keep the parties focused on content, while managing their interpersonal relationships.

As these techniques are applied, the parties reach closure, which we will cover in the next chapter.

Chapter 10

Closure

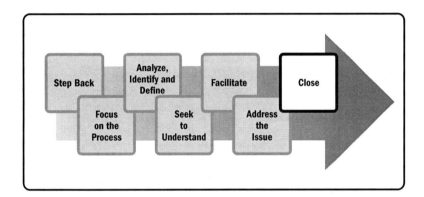

Chapter overview

In conflicts, closure is the agreement (tacit or explicit) among the parties. Closure is the part of the process where the parties agree that the debate or negotiation is over and on how they will handle things going forward.

In this chapter, we address closure in terms of the following subjects:

- When and how to escalate—bringing about closure by engaging outside intervention;
- The nature of arbitration and authority based decisions;
- Agreeing to disagree;
- Real and false closure;
- Communicating the results;
- Taking action; and
- Process assessment.

Closure

Closure implies a resolution in the form of an agreement. Not all disputes are resolved. In some cases, conflicts last for years or more and are never fully resolved, though there may be many disputes within the conflict that are resolved.

In projects and business in general, we usually need concrete resolution, as quickly as possible, with minimal use of participants' time and effort. When the parties cannot agree upon a solution, even after outside facilitation, and there is no higher authority to impose one on them, usually it means that it may be time for a hiatus from the conflict (allowing time for the parties to calm down and reflect), compromise, accommodation, litigation or an agreement to disagree. When the parties agree to disagree, there is closure, at least until the issue comes up again.

Fortunately, in organizations, there is usually an authority to go to for arbitration or authority based decision making. It might be a supervisor or manager who has authority over the parties or someone who has been assigned as the arbiter of a particular type of dispute, for example an architectural board or a subject matter expert.

While there is usually a higher authority, generally seek to avoid escalating disputes for authority decisions and, if you have authority, hold off on using it.

Escalation—Intervention

There are two meanings for the term *escalation* in conflict management. One is the intensification of the conflict and the severity of the techniques used in addressing it. The other refers to bringing the conflict to higher authority for resolution or to seek mediation or facilitation. There is a relationship between these two meanings. Intensity escalation is a sign that outside intervention may be necessary.

As we said in the chapter on Process, the parties define how they will address the conflict. The approach may be part of a communication plan or a clause in a contract or tacit agreement based on a long history of conflict management. The plan should include criteria and protocols to define how the parties will determine whether they will escalate, what escalation approaches (mediation/facilitation or arbitration) they will use, who they will go to and in what order.

When to Escalate

In a project situation, there can be a time limit set as a dispute arises and is recognized. The parties might agree to try to work things out themselves within the limit and then escalate. The duration of the limit depends on the nature of the dispute and its time criticality.

With or without time pressures, the parties and other conflict stakeholders can look for telltale signs of the need to reach out. These are some of the common signs: (1) circular arguments (going over the same ground multiple times); (2) rising tensions and emotional outbursts caused by frustration; (3) a recognition that the parties are stuck in their positions and have no way forward; (4) frequent tangents or bouncing from detail to overview and back again without resolving anything; (5) time pressures as deadlines are approaching. If the conflicting parties are aware and skilled, they will be the ones to initiate escalation. If, on the other hand, they are lost in debate, then it may be another stakeholder who escalates, forcing the parties to "look up" from their arguments and address the conflict more effectively.

How to Escalate

When the time for escalation is at hand, make sure you don't surprise others by going to your boss or that person's boss, or to the general public. Make sure escalation is a conscious decision that all parties are at least aware of. Note that it is <u>not</u> necessary to get everyone to agree to escalate, but everyone should be aware that escalation is taking place.

If there is unilateral escalation, it will generally cause a degree of anger, disappointment, or distrust in the other parties. Think of how you would feel if your boss tells you that he or she has been asked to intervene by the boss of the one who has escalated the issue. It is likely to make you look bad in the eyes of your boss, who is most likely to be surprised by the escalation. You are likely to have the sense that the other party has been dishonest and manipulative. Unilateral escalation is a sign that the communication among the parties has broken down.

It is a whole other thing if the other party comes to you and tells you that she thinks you have reached a point at which escalation is needed, and that with or without your consent (which she would like to have) she is going to bring the issue to higher authority to seek a decision. It gives you a chance to see if you can change her mind and a chance to inform your boss that there is an issue he is going to become involved with.

Once the escalation is announced or agreed upon, it is necessary to inform the intervening parties about the nature of the conflict and what you would like them to do.

In a complex conflict, you will have likely addressed and documented the nature of the conflict, its environment, and the parties' positions, wants, needs and common objectives as well as decision criteria and their weights. Clearly identify areas of agreement and disagreement.

If these have not been addressed in an orderly way, then address them before you escalate. By doing so, you may come to a resolution yourselves. If you cannot address them because of emotional issues or poor communication, then engage a mediator or facilitator before escalating to arbitration. If the other party is unwilling to consider mediation then you may have to escalate that procedural conflict for an authority intervention before you seek resolution of the content conflict.

If these elements have been addressed, then make sure there is sufficient documentation to permit the intervening party(ies) to become familiar with the situation. If possible, make sure the documentation content is mutually agreed upon by the parties. The intervening party will probably want to discuss the issues with each of the parties, separately and/or together.

Mediation vs. Arbitration

Escalation may be for mediation or arbitration. Mediation or facilitation is intervention by people who do not have the authority to resolve the issues. They are discussed in the chapter Facilitate Rapport.

Escalating to bring in a mediator means that the parties have recognized the need for help in collaborating and negotiating. Mediation is a step taken to help the parties come to closure while avoiding arbitration.

Arbitration—Authority Based Decisions

Arbitration is an escalation in which the people in conflict agree to be bound by the decision of a third party or tribunal. We will use the term broadly to include litigation and escalation for decisions by people at higher levels of authority, as well as formal arbitration.

Arbitration is needed when the principle parties cannot reach agreement within a reasonable time limit.

In formal arbitration the parties agree upon the arbitrator(s). Commonly, each party chooses a member of an arbitration tribunal and the two arbitrators choose a third. The parties present their positions and arguments with more or less formal discussion, and the tribunal decides. The tribunal's decision is binding on the participants.

Litigation is another alternative. The parties agree to take the decision making to the courts. It is considered a last resort, as it is expensive and time consuming and often results in compromise resolutions that satisfy neither party.

If projects and the conflicts in them are managed well, it is less likely that formal arbitration and litigation will be needed. With effective project management mutually agreed upon objectives and expectations, clear contracts and effective communication will help to avoid unnecessary conflicts, raise the necessary ones at the right time, and have an effective conflict management process to handle them. With effective conflict management, the parties will use their skills to come to consensus or escalate to minimize unnecessary effort and time.

Using Authority—Informal Arbitration in Projects

In many project disputes, there is a natural arbitrator or arbitration board. When planning your projects, decide up front about who has the authority to make binding decisions regarding specific topics. Recognize the hierarchy and its implied arbitrators. In this form of arbitration, the people in conflict do not get to choose the arbitrator(s). They do get to decide (within constraints) when to escalate the issue.

As an authority figure, you have the responsibility to make decisions _and_ to facilitate agreement among peers.

As a manager, it is often difficult to hold back from just mandating a decision and being done with it. "Why spend the time and effort to allow for a consensus decision?" you might ask. Because you want (1) the disputants to 'own' the solution to improve the probability of successful application, and (2) to make your job easier by having subordinates settle their own disputes within their scopes of control.

This second motivator may engender fear in some. "What happens to me if they get really good at this conflict management stuff and make really good decisions without me?" If as a manager, you do yourself out of a job by cultivating those who work for you, then you are valuable as a manager. If you keep making the decisions and holding on to your expert knowledge, you <u>may</u> be a valuable subject matter asset but not a valuable manager. Even as a subject matter expert, you are more valuable to your organization if you collaborate with others.

As we pointed out in discussing hierarchies and the strength of consensus decisions, authority based decision making has an important place in conflict management. It is a means for having highly qualified people make informed decisions to minimize the time and effort required and promote quality results. As with all powerful things, authority decision making has a dark side. Arbitrarily imposed decisions may lead to sub-optimal resolutions.

As "the boss,' you can reserve the right or have the responsibility to review and approve any decision made by your subordinates. If this is part of your conflict management process, then make sure that your criteria are known to the parties before they address the conflict. If you find yourself reversing decisions regularly question your open-mindedness as well as the needs of the other parties to improve their skills.

Agreeing to Disagree

It is best to avoid escalation and to resolve the issue at the peer level. One way to avoid escalation is by agreeing to disagree. For example, in a conflict over a poor performance review if there is no agreement, the review and the challenge to it both stand on the record. In a conflict over some perceived insult, if there is no apology and no acceptance that the insult was in fact not one at all, then the issue may be brushed under the rug, perhaps forgotten; perhaps not. In the case of a dispute between a vendor and client, the two may choose to disengage instead of litigating.

Unresolved issues have a tendency to reappear, particularly if the resolution is needed to move a project forward or to settle personal issues.

Are You Sure? Real and False Closure

With or without escalation the parties can reach a conclusion. But, just because someone says they agree, doesn't mean that they *really* agree.

Coming to a resolution requires that each party acknowledge their agreement. Of course; that is obvious. Yet we find that some disputes reappear after the parties have each acknowledged their agreement and sometimes the agreed upon follow up action is never done.

Some agreements are real and represent a commitment; others are just for the moment. Between these, all shades of gray, as there are varying degrees of commitment and reversibility.

The agreements that are just for the moment may be tactics to delay a real decision to gain advantage for one's side. They may also be indications of fear at a point in the negotiation that causes one to 'cave in' to avoid further conflict, even though not convinced. When the fear subsides, the conflict reemerges. A false closure may occur because the parties failed to consider uncertainty and risk and change into the future. They agreed on something that was win-win at the time of the agreement but when change arises one of the parties perceives that he has lost and may reopen the conflict.

The accommodating, avoiding, and passive-aggressive conflict management styles tend to lead to false closure. Remember the Trip to Abilene and how quickly the parties repudiated their agreement.

Example—Reopening Agreements

In the absolute sense, there is no such thing as a totally permanent agreement, just like there is no such thing as a totally firm decision. Agreements and decisions, like everything else, are subject to change.

For example, in a conflict regarding a fixed price contract, the parties agreed that it was fair to have a price that was settled in advance with the stipulation that changes would be negotiated in good faith. Not far into the project, it was clear to the vendor that the client was making many changes and that the scope of the project was growing. Going to the client with this news, the client put her foot down and said that a fixed price is a fixed price and that the changes were not anything out of the ordinary.

Here we have gone from an agreement to a conflict about something the parties thought was settled in their negotiations. When this happens there may be loss of trust. Neither party can tell whether the other party is being callous, greedy, and consciously unfair or that they really believe in their stated position. In the case of greedy, the choices are unpleasant. The client or the vendor could walk away from the project. One or the other can give in, even knowing that they are being taken advantage of. This can lead to poor performance and a break in relations that will impact future projects.

What Can You Do About False Closure?

What does this kind of closure do for project morale and commitment? How does it feel? What impact might it have on behavior? What does it cost the organization in rework, turnover and productivity loss? The answers to these questions depend on your environment and situation.

What can you do to help to ensure real closure? Unfortunately, there is no sure cure. But, you can influence the situation in a number of ways.

First, make sure you are clear in your own mind about your decision to agree and resolve to be honest with the others regarding your intentions.

Then, early on, discuss closure and strength of agreement as part of your process definition. Awareness of the real-false closure issue can help to ensure that the parties address reversibility, uncertainty and other relevant aspects of the conflict that affect the strength of the agreement.

You may use a technique that is part of the U.S. criminal justice system, where a person who is admitting to a crime must not only say that they did it but also fully describe what it is that they did and how they did it. In our project conflict context, this translates to having each of the parties say what they are agreeing to in sufficient detail to give themselves and the other parties a sense of their conviction. This may be done in writing as part of the process to arrive at a mutual statement of the agreement or orally in the case of minor or less important and informally handled disputes.

The next section addresses conviction and may be a useful topic for discussion as you set the tone for conflict management with the other parties.

Conviction

Reaching strong, lasting agreement involves conviction; you should be relatively convinced of the effectiveness of the resolution before agreeing to it. What does it mean to be convinced of something? To convince is "To bring by the use of argument or evidence to firm belief or a course of action" (Convince, n.d.). Firm belief does not necessarily mean complete, unquestioned belief though it does imply a strong sense that the belief or agreement or course of action is correct based on a set of assumptions that are well enough founded on fact and logic to make it seem that they are true. The difference between blind belief conviction and strong conviction is a significant factor in conflict management. The more an individual is convinced of his or her position, the more he or she will hold to it.

There is a paradox. You need conviction to argue your points and satisfy your needs, it motivates you to be an effective participant in the search for the optimal resolution. At the same time, people, can be too convinced or convinced too soon. They may start out convinced that they are right, that their position is totally true and must prevail. They debate to promote and defend their position by offering up positive arguments and refuting or ignoring opposing ones.

Imagine if everyone came to every conflict totally convinced that they were right. Life would be a continuous flow of irreconcilable or win-lose conflicts; every conflict a zero-sum game. It is unpleasant and unproductive.

Keep an open mind. Listen. Remember the difference between your position, interests, wants, and needs. There may be alternatives that are equal to or superior to yours. Have you spent enough time in dialogue and cognitive analysis to understand the problem and the desired ends before fixating on the means. Have you explored your assumptions?

"Dispassionate objectivity is itself a passion, for the real and for the truth."— Abraham Maslow

Question everything, even your most dearly held beliefs and opinions. If your beliefs aren't tested how can you know if they are worth keeping?

At the same time, beware of being ineffective or indecisive. Overdoing analytical questioning leads to chronic doubt and that leads to an inability to commit your full efforts to the implementation of the decision. The right balance is hard to describe. You must subjectively evaluate your sense of conviction, having objectively evaluated the situation from multiple perspectives.

Communicating the Results

Once a conflict is resolved, there are people who have a need to know the resolution. The parties to the conflict are responsible for communicating their resolution and the reasons behind it. Depending on the situation, this can be done with varying degrees of formality.

As a rule, it is best to put the resolution in writing, even if it is just a simple email confirming what has been decided. Putting it in writing has powerful effects: (1) writing requires the effort to accurately communicate one's thoughts; (2) it enables the parties to agree to more than just words in the air. They agree to a documented conclusion. They have an opportunity to edit and make sure they really have gotten to a meeting of the minds; and (3) It makes transmitting the decision to others easier.

The written statement can come out of the process of reaching agreement. As the parties state their understanding, a mutual statement emerges.

Going into the conflict, consider and decide as part of your process how you will communicate the results. How much detailed background information, how formal a presentation, who will keep the notes, who will write up the results and how will they be validated before they are released?

While you want to avoid unnecessary documentation, some is needed. Documenting the conflict as we move through the process puts you in a good position to periodically get a sense of progress and makes escalation easier, given the need to communicate the current state of the conflict to intervening parties.

Taking Action

In projects, action is the main point. Conflicts result in decisions and decisions result in action (which includes not taking action). Actualizing the decision is the real test of conflict resolution. If the parties have reached agreement and then do not follow through, they have <u>not</u> really resolved anything.

As part of the resolution, make sure there is an action plan, the next steps required to implement the decision.

As action is taken, there is need for a continuous assessment of the results and openness to re-explore the resolution. If the results do not meet expectations or in the face of change there may be a need to reopen the issue. Openness to reassessment is a clear indication that the parties understand the difference between blindly believing that their resolution is perfect and understanding that change is a fact.

Assessing the Process

Process assessment is the means for achieving the goals of building and maintaining healthy relationships, personal growth and promoting continuous process improvement. Whether you call them project performance reviews, post mortems, lessons learned sessions or process reviews, they should be held to enable process improvement to optimize performance.

Both at closure and during performance, step back and evaluate the conflict management process. Reviews may take place at the end of a conflict, periodically over time to assess the management of multiple conflicts, or as part of project performance review. Ask the following questions:

- Did your original communication plan serve its purpose?
- Was it followed?
- What changes would you want to make going forward?
- Were there issues and outbursts that need to be explored to resolve lingering hurts?
- How do we *feel* about the experience? Was it pleasant, productive, etc.?
- Was the right media available and used in the most effective ways?
- Were data available and used during the process?
- Was there healthy rapport? Did the parties listen actively? Was there mutual respect? Open mindedness?
- Were the right communication and decision-making tools and techniques used? How did they work out? What have you learned?
- Was an escalation or intervention required and, if so why and how well did it go? What have you learned?
- Can we identify any trends or styles of behavior, positive or negative, across multiple conflicts? Do the same conflicts occur over and over again? Do they have to?
- Is there sufficient documentation?
- How can we improve the process?

Depending on the circumstances, the assessment may be a brief informal discussion among the parties. For example, "You know, when we started to address this issue I thought we would never be able to agree, but I want to acknowledge our ability to communicate clearly, be open to one another's ideas and to find a resolution that seems to satisfy both of us. I think it is a lot better than the one I started with."

If there were flaws in the process then the assessment would include a statement like, "We had a bit of a struggle with that _____ issue. How could we avoid that kind of thing in the future?"

More formally, the assessment may be performed by the participants, with or without a facilitator, using a checklist of questions, like the ones above, regarding how conflict management principles and best practices were applied.

There may be resistance to assessing performance and behavior. Some find it threatening and others a waste of time. Get over these attitudes. Transparency and process assessment are musts if you want to thrive. Even if you can't get the group to do it, do it yourself.

Assessment should reflect on your goals: Did you reach an optimal solution? Are relationships healthy? Was there personal growth?, Is the process improving?

Recap: Closure

This chapter has addressed closure and, in the context of process assessment, a recap of the conflict management approach.

Closure exists when there is agreement on a resolution. The agreement may be to disagree. Closure can be aided through escalation to higher authority for arbitration or by engaging an outside facilitator or mediator. Escalation does not mean that the parties have failed in any way. It means they have not been able to come to an agreement themselves.

Healthy closure implies agreement in which the parties are convinced that their resolution is one that satisfies objectives. Conviction leads to commitment. Be convinced because the arguments are founded on logic and fact not blind belief. Keep your mind open. Remember, agreements are always subject to change and that there is a continuum of reversible to irreversible decisions.

Communicate the results in writing. Let the complexity of the results and the needs of the environment dictate the writing requirements. A consistent and accurate statement of the decision and its implications and rationale is very often a requirement in projects and organizations.

Take action. Monitor results and adjust as needed.

Assess the conflict management process to learn as an organization and as individuals.

Chapter 11

Conclusion

Since conflict management is a process, it really has no end. It continues across projects and as multiple conflicts within projects. That is why process review is so important. In this final chapter, we will recap definitions and key points as a framework for you to use for assessing your conflict management process with an eye towards improvement on two levels: (1) your own process as applied to individual conflict events; and (2) your organization's process, given your ability to influence it.

Definitions: Conflict and Conflict Management

Conflict is disagreement between people with different perceptions, ideas, needs, or interests. It is inevitable in projects and in any relationship. Conflict can be an opportunity to reach an agreement that improves on the positions of the parties or an opportunity to win out over the competition. In projects, conflicts must be resolved quickly, with minimal effort and with optimal resolutions that further the project's success. Many conflicts can be considered as tasks on a critical path. At the same time, rushing to resolve conflicts or moving so fast as to postpone or avoid them when they naturally arise in project life can be just as damaging as taking an inordinately long time to resolve them.

When conflict isn't present take it as a sign that something may be wrong. Avoid unnecessary conflict, but proactively promote conflict at the right times in project life and make each conflict event a perfect example of the work of a master conflict manager.

Conflict Management is the process of applying skills, tools, and techniques to achieve the goals of

- optimal solutions,
- healthy relationships,
- personal growth, and
- continuous improvement in the way conflict is managed.

It is a foundation skill that is essential to the health and performance of any relationship based organization, project, process or system.

Conflict management addresses conflict content and the relationships among the parties. It requires blending analytical, linear thinking and non-linear, holistic, creative thinking. Effective conflict management promotes seeing the big picture and the details and appreciation of the complex nature of people interacting over disagreements. Conflict management requires open-minded objectivity and the ability to be mindfully aware of every aspect of the situation. Moment to moment mindfulness of everything that is going on in and around you helps you to avoid reactive behavior and do what is right for the situation at hand. Reactive behavior tends to transform content disputes into relationship-based conflicts.

Conflict management is too complex for a cookbook solution. It requires an adaptive approach that blends principles and techniques within a consciously managed process. There is need for a framework and good practices and concepts that can be adapted for each situation.

General Approach and Process

Take a practical, analytically objective approach to conflict while addressing the human side with its communications, emotions, behaviors, motivations, and uncertainty.

The overall approach in this book recognizes that there are many variations of conflicts within and around projects, that there is a wide variety of people with unique motivations, values, styles, skills, experience, mental models, etc., and a wide variety of organizations, each with its own motivations, style, policies, values, culture, etc.

Figure 11-1 has been used throughout the book to maintain a connection among the steps in the process and the techniques and principles used in them. It is a

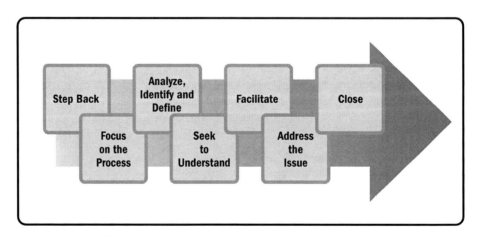

Figure 11-1: The conflict management process

reminder that while there is a process it is complex and nonlinear with steps that overlap and affect one another. The steps are:

- Step back and assess your personal condition: your goals, emotions, expectations, conflict management skill and style, etc. Apply open-minded mindfulness. Get centered and be ready for anything.
- Focus on the process to develop a conflict management plan as a part of your communication plan. Start with organization wide norms, policies, and procedures, refine them and adapt them to your project and then to each conflict situation;
- Analyze to identify and define the conflict and its environment, history, dynamics, issues and parties' positions, interests, needs and desires, and objectives;
- Seek to understand the parties' values and mental models;
- Facilitate rapport, an appropriate atmosphere, or climate, by addressing fear, anger, communication, and trust issues;
- Address the issue at hand to seek an optimal resolution while using the right tools and techniques and being mindful of reactive behavior; and
- Close the conflict or dispute with an authentic agreement, even if it is an agreement to disagree, an action plan, follow-through, and process evaluation.

Understanding the Conflict and Its Nature

We take an analytical approach that enables the parties, collectively as a group facing the conflict or as individuals, to know as much about the conflict as possible. Analysis is done to choose the right tools and techniques to manage the conflict. Following is a recap that identifies the categories, types and attributes we discussed in the book.

Common Types of Projects

The common types of conflicts that occur in projects are discussed in the chapter Conflicts in Projects

- Schedule conflicts
- Priorities conflicts
- Resource conflicts
- Technical conflicts
- Administrative procedures conflicts
- Personality conflicts
- Cost conflicts
- Performance conflicts
- Supplier selection conflicts

These occur across the project life cycle and between stakeholders at different levels in the hierarchy and with varying degrees of authority.

Attributes of a Conflict

To have sufficient information to decide how best to manage your conflicts, define them in terms of the following attributes, discussed in the Chapter 5, Analysis: The Nature of a Conflict:

- Subject and causes;
- The number of parties and their interests, needs, positions and wants;
- Criteria (values, priorities) that will be used to decide on the question in conflict;
- Organizational issues—context in terms of inter group, inter organizational, etc.;
- Authority and hierarchy—are the direct parties on the same level?
- Category—content or relationship (emotion) centered
- Complexity—makes conflicts difficult to manage. The number of parties and organizations, legal and cross-organizational relationships, diversity, number of stakeholders, and combinations of the other attributes contribute to complexity. In addition, the following attributes also contribute to complexity
  - Intensity—How heated is the conflict? Are emotions on the surface?
  - Intractability—How resistant to resolution is the conflict?
  - Importance—To what degree does the success of the project rely on an optimal resolution?
  - Time pressure—How quickly is a resolution needed? Increased time pressure contributes to intensity.
  - Certainty and Uncertainty—To what degree can you be sure of the outcome of applying the resolution?
  - Irreversibility—How easy is it to change the decision?
  - Competitiveness—How likely are the parties to be competitive as opposed to collaborative?

Seeking to Understand Yourself and Others

People and their relationships are at the heart of conflict management. Self-knowledge and knowledge of others come from being objectively mindful. Objectivity and mindfulness enable you to see your emotional responses as they arise and to see how others are taking effect from things you say and do. Add awareness of cultural norms and acceptance of the fact that you are responsible for your emotions and the behaviors they elicit to the mix to set a solid foundation for applying conflict management techniques.

Competencies and Techniques

With knowledge of the nature of the conflict and the people involved in it, you can apply the right techniques with the right degree of formality. The following techniques are applied in managing conflict. The choice of technique and the way it is applied depends on the specific nature of the conflict.

- Cognitive analysis to determine the nature of the conflict, its setting and the parties and their positions, interests, needs and wants;
- Process management and engineering—defining and refining the conflict management process
- Insight or mindfulness meditation—enabling effective facilitation, communication and self control using breath and body awareness to be present, mindful and concentrated, centered and responsive as opposed to reactive
- Communication management, facilitation, and mediation—building and maintaining rapport using facilitation and mediation skills to enable the sharing of information required to reach agreement. Six facilitation techniques are:
  1. Active listening—taking the effort to hear and understand what others are saying
  2. Questioning—enabling active listening by digging into the other parties communication and making sure your understanding is accurate
  3. Matching and Mirroring—creating a sense of trust and comfort
  4. Using body language—going beyond the words
  5. Making eye contact—maintaining trust and comfort
  6. Moderating the communication process—managing the flow of communication.
- Diversity awareness—understanding cultural, thinking style and conflict management style differences and managing them to avoid and better handle conflicts.
- Situational management—understanding and flexing your conflict management style and your process to the needs of each situation
- Dialogue—exploring issues with no other objective than to gain understanding
- Debate—arguing for your point and against competing points to convince others
- Decision making—applying analytical techniques, such as the weights and scores method, to reach agreement
- Negotiating—conferring with others to reach agreement
- Escalation—taking the conflict to higher authority or bringing in outside help to reach agreement, including the agreement to disagree
- Putting it in writing—documenting interim results and final decisions to enhance clarity and promote follow through on the decisions associated with conflict resolution
- Assessing performance—reviewing the way you manage conflict both for individual conflicts and across multiple conflicts to enable continuous improvement.

Putting it All Together

Combining all of these elements into a unified process is moreof an art than a science.

It is like learning to ski, surf, or ride a bicycle, only far more complex.

You learn the mechanics, do it and learn from experience until the mechanics become fully integrated into a fluid process. After a while, you don't have to consciously think so much about doing it, yet you are present, alert, precise and able to respond and adapt. You continue to get better by assessing your own performance and getting input from others.

These are the foundations for success:

- Stay centered—calm, cool and collected, ready for anything;
- Be mindful of your sense of self, your feelings, needs, wants, reactions and positions
- Be fully engaged in finding optimal resolutions, healthy relationships, personal growth, and continuous improvement.

References

Al-Tabtabai, H., Alex, A. P., & Abou-alfotouh, A. (2001). Conflict resolution using cognitive analysis approach. *Project Management Journal, 32*(2), 4–16.

Bohm, D. (1996). *On dialogue.* London, England: Routledge.

Box, G. E. P., & Draper, N. R. (1987). *Empirical model-building and response surfaces* (p. 424). New York, NY: Wiley.

Brown, S. T., III. (n.d.). *Conflict management in projects.* Retrieved from http://www .globalknowledge.com/training/generic.asp?pageid=1644&country=United+ States

Conflict Research Consortium. (1998). Intractable conflict, confusing interests (what you really want) with positions (what you say you want). Retrieved from http:// www.colorado.edu/conflict/peace/problem/intpos-p.htm

Conflict Research Consortium. (2000). Article summary of "Intractable Conflict" by Peter W. Coleman. In Morton Deutsch and Peter T. Coleman, (Eds.), *The handbook of conflict resolution: Theory and practice* San Francisco, Ca: Jossey-Bass Publishers, 2000, pp. 428–450. Retrieved from http://www.crinfo.org/index.jsp

Contest. (n.d.) Retrieved from http://www.merriam-webster.com/netdict/contest

Convince. (n.d.). Retrieved from http://www.thefreedictionary.com/convinced

Covey, S. (2004). *The 7 habits of highly effective people.* New York, NY: Free Press.

Cummings, H. W., Long, L. W., & Lewis, M. L. (1983). *Managing communication in organizations: An introduction.* Dubuque, IA: Gorsuch Scarisbrick Publishers.

Davenport, T. (2008, January 7). Why Six Sigma Is on the Downslope [Web log post]. Retrieved from http://blogs.hbr.org/davenport/2008/01/why_six_sigma_ is_on_the_downsl.html Harvard Business Review Blog, "Why Six Sigma is On the Downslope" by Thomas Davenport.

Dialogue. (n.d.a). Retrieved from http://www.co-intelligence.org/P-dialogue.html

Dialogue. (n.d.b). Retrieved from wordnetweb.princeton.edu/perl/webwn

Fisher, R., & Ury, W. (1981). *Getting to yes: Negotiating agreement without giving in* (pp. 155–159). New York, NY: 1981, Penguin Books.

Ford, J. (2001). *Cross cultural conflict resolution in teams.* Retrieved from http://www.mediate .com/articles/ford5.cfm

Gladwell, M. (2005). *Blink: The power of thinking without thinking.* New York, NY: 2005, Little Brown And Company, Time Warner Book Group.

Harvey, J. B. (1988). *The Abilene paradox: The management of agreement, organizational dynamics* (pp. 17–43. New York, NY: American Management Association.

Hofstede, G., & Geert, J. (2005). *Cultures and organizations: Software of the mind.* New York, NY: McGraw-Hill.

Hollnagel, E. (2004). *Barriers and accident prevention.* Aldershot, UK: Ashgate Publishing, 2004, p. 147.

Kaufman, S., Elliott, M., & Shmueli, D. (2003). Frames, framing and reframing, beyond intractability, Version II. Retrieved from http://www.crinfo.org/framing.htm

Lazarus, L. (n.d.). *A conversation with professor Leonard Riskin about mindfulness, dispute resolution, and mindfulness resources for mediators.* Retrieved from http://mediate.com/articles/lazarusl4.cfm

Nair, S., & Balasubramania, M. (2008, December). *The role of emotional intelligence in organisational leadership.* Paper presented at the Sixth AIMS International Conference on Management, p. 408.

Open-mindedness. (n.d.). In Wiktionary. Retrieved from http://en.wiktionary.org/wiki/open-minded

Pitagorsky, G. (2000). *PM basics.* New York, NY: International Institute for Learning.

Pitagorsky, G. (2001). Conflict – opportunity for relationship building and effective decision. In J. Knutson (Ed.), *Project management for the business professional: A comprehensive guide* (pp. 418–439). New York, NY: Wiley and Sons.

Project Management Institute. (2004). *A guide to the project management body of knowledge (PMBOK® guide)* (3rd ed.). Newtown Square, PA: Project Management Institute.

Project Management Institute. (2008). *A guide to the project management body of knowledge (PMBOK® guide)* (4th ed.). Newtown Square, PA: Project Management Institute.

Ramsey, R. D. (1996). Conflict resolution skills for supervisors. *Supervision, 57*(8), 6–7. Retrieved from http://www.allbusiness.com/human-resources/workforce-management-conflict-resolution/575374-1.html

Scheinkopf, L. (1999). *Thinking for a change.* Boca Raton, FL: St. Lucie Press.

Senge, P., Kleiner, A., Roberts, C., Ross, R., & Smith, B. (1994). *The fifth discipline.* New York, NY: Crown Business.

Thamhain, H., & Wilemon, D. (1975). Conflict management in project life cycles. Sloan Management Review, 16(3), 31–50.

Thomas, K., & Kilman, R., (n.d.). Thomas Kilman conflict mode instrument. Retrieved from http://www.shropshirevts.com/docs/thomaskilmanconflictinstrumentq.pdf

Verma, Vijay, K. (1996). *Human resource skills for the project manager* (p. 118). Newtown Square, PA. Project Management Institute.

Appendix A

Determining Complexity

Complexity is one of the attributes of a conflict.

The following method is relatively simple and arbitrary. It is meant as a means to give you an analytical sense of your conflict's complexity. You don't need the numbers at all. You can analyze by just considering the attributes or you can be more formal and use a rating method. Rate the items based on group consensus or on your own subjective opinion.

Remember, analysis is a means for stepping back to better understand a conflict. Stepping back enables objectivity and that provides an advantage in finding win-win resolutions.

Approach

1. Rank each seven conflict attributes on a scale of high (3), medium (2), and low (1) and add the items to get a relative sense of the complexity of the conflict.

   The seven attributes that contribute to the eighth (complexity) are these:
   - Intensity—How heated is the conflict?
   - Intractability—How resistant to resolution is the conflict?
   - Importance—To what degree does the success of the project rely on an optimal resolution?
   - Time pressure—How quickly is a resolution needed?
   - Certainty and Uncertainty—To what degree can you be sure of the outcome of applying the resolution?
   - Reversibility—How easy is it to change the decision?
   - Competitiveness—How likely are the parties to be competitive as opposed to collaborative?
2. Rank the conflict in terms of its category, on a scale from **completely focused on content** (1) to highly relationship centered and emotional (5).
3. Multiply the sum of the complexity attributes by the category ranking.
4. Multiply the result by the factor for number of directly involved parties:
   - Two participants: (1)
   - 3–5: (2)
   - Greater than 5: (3).

5. Multiply by the hierarchy factor: (1) no hierarchy among the direct parties, or (2) hierarchies or authority differences.

6. Multiply that result by a ranking of organizational issues (see the Chapter 2, Conflict in Projects):
   - Intrapersonal (1)
   - Interpersonal (1)
   - Intragroup (1)
   - Intergroup (2)
   - Intraorganizational (3)
   - Interorganizational (4).

The result is a relative score of your conflict's complexity. The higher the number, the more likely you need to make sure that there is a well-defined process and some facilitation or mediation. The highest score is 2520, but if you have a score of over 60 and only two participants from the same group with no hierarchies, consider your conflict to be complex.

The numbers are just an indication. The important thing is to remember to assess the nature of the conflict so you can identify areas that you need to focus on to make the resolution as effective as possible.

The greater the complexity, the greater the need for more formal conflict management.